"April Cassidy has written  id
message. In fact, I asked e-
ported to me, 'I am whol is
book. She addresses the i. m
Ephesians 5:33. Also, she delves into submission and challenges her fellow women to rethink the word *submission* and what it should really
look like in their lives. She is open and honest about how she thought
she was a "good wife" but realized, after reading the *Love and Respect*
book that you wrote, what she had overlooked. April does an excellent
job of placing a mirror in front of readers so that they may see the
ways they have been disrespectful, but she also provides a comforting
hug as she explains how the disrespect can end and a life of respecting
one's husband can move into place. She provides great insight into her
own struggles and a wonderful chapter where her own husband gives
his thoughts on her transformation. April challenges, encourages, and
breathes hope for all wives. I feel like this is a companion book to *Love
and Respect*. There is something about receiving advice from someone
who has walked the same path as you, in the same high heels perhaps.'"
—EMERSON EGGERICHS, author of *Love and Respect*

"April knows what it's like to struggle in her marriage with frustration
and anger toward her spouse. Her journey to becoming a peaceful wife
will resonate with any reader who wants new peace in her own marriage. I love that this book walks each of us through the reality checks
we need in order to have the marriage we want!"
—SHAUNTI FELDHAHN, social researcher and
best-selling author of *For Women Only*

"*The Peaceful Wife* is a must-read for every bride who wants to arm
her marriage in the spiritual battle! April Cassidy offers her own beautiful story of awakening to God's design for marriage and calls us all
to humbly embrace the help of His Holy Spirit. Her writing is well
grounded in Scripture and filled with eye-opening wisdom, testimonies, and checklists to help me and every wife excel at honoring God by
respecting our husbands."
—JENNIFER O. WHITE, author of *Prayers for New
Brides* and *Marriage Armor for the Praying Bride*

April Cassidy

The Peaceful Wife

LIVING IN SUBMISSION TO

Christ AS Lord

Kregel
Publications

The Peaceful Wife: Living in Submission to Christ as Lord
© 2016 by April Cassidy

Published by Kregel Publications, a division of Kregel, Inc., 2450 Oak Industrial Drive NE, Grand Rapids, MI 49505.

The author and publisher are not engaged in rendering medical or psychological services, and this book is not intended as a guide to diagnose or treat medical or psychological problems. If medical, psychological, or other expert assistance is required by the reader, please seek the services of your own health care provider or certified counselor.

Personal stories have been used by permission. In some cases, names and identifying details have been changed to protect the privacy of the individuals involved.

All Scripture quotations are from the Holy Bible, New International Version®, NIV®. Copyright © 1973, 1978, 1984, 2011 by Biblica, Inc.™ Used by permission of Zondervan. All rights reserved worldwide. www.zondervan.com

ISBN 978-0-8254-4394-7

Printed in the United States of America

20 21 22 23 24 25 / 5 4 3 2

I dedicate this book to my loving husband, Greg. I am so thankful for your patience with me as I stumbled along trying to understand what on earth it meant to be a godly wife. Thank you for offering such a beautiful example of the grace, mercy, forgiveness, and unconditional love of Christ to me. I thank and praise God for what He has done in each of us and in our marriage. I certainly could not have done any of this on my own. What a blessing to me that God allowed us to share this narrow path together.

Contents

Preface. 9
Introduction 13

1. Our Story 17
2. Finding the Missing Piece of the Puzzle 27
3. Let's Be Honest 37
4. The Absolute Lordship of Christ 59
5. God's Beautiful Design 78
6. Recognizing Disrespect 105
7. Acknowledging Our Sin 120
8. My Husband Shares His Heart 136
9. Learning the Language of Respect. 147
10. A Smorgasbord of Respect. 168
11. Communicating Our Desires Respectfully 187
12. Respecting Our Husbands During Conflict. 215
13. Sharing the Journey 235

Appendix: Reaching a Husband Who Doesn't
    Know Christ 245
Notes 259
For Further Study. 261
About the Author 263

Preface

I am now a very happily married Christian mother of two, part-time pharmacist, and Christian marriage blogger. Sharing God's design for marriage with women is my greatest passion. In this book, I want to explore some things with you that I wish I had been exposed to before Greg and I ever got married. My prayer is that God might use my experiences to help you avoid some of my painful, self-defeating mistakes and find His life-giving, beautiful wisdom instead. I am not a professional counselor, psychologist, pastor, minister, psychiatrist, or seminary-trained "expert." I am a wife who loves God wholeheartedly and who wants to relate my personal, life-changing experience with Jesus Christ and the Bible.

I write from the perspective of a wife who was formerly strong willed, controlling, bossy, perfectionistic, people pleasing, overly responsible, overly "helpful," and dominating with a passive, unplugged husband. I must write from what I know, from my own story and experiences. In the process, I am excited to share some other wives' stories as well. God has allowed me the honor and privilege of watching Him transform hundreds of women and their marriages through my blog at www.peacefulwife.com. Although God's Word applies to all marriages and all situations, this book will probably be most helpful for wives whose marriage dynamics fall into this general category of a dominant wife married to a passive husband.

Wives who are rather timid, overly submissive, or passive may need to approach biblical concepts about being a godly wife from a different angle. They may need to learn to speak up more and to be bolder, for instance. We each have our own worldview, personality, and personal history that help to shape the way we filter what we read. I want to be up front about my particular slant so that my words might be most helpful to the greatest number of women.

I fervently desire to honor God with every word I write. I pray that each believer will carefully weigh what I write against Scripture. I am human and prone to error, after all. The Bible is the only source of absolute truth. Our job as followers of Christ is to love and obey Jesus; He handles the results.

One book doesn't begin to give me enough space to share all that there is to know about becoming a godly wife, but I am excited to get to share a bit with you. I pray that God might richly bless your walk with Him and your marriage as you prayerfully read through these pages. I pray that God might use me to point you toward Jesus as both Savior and Lord and toward the wisdom of His Word. I pray for you, my precious new friend, to experience the supernatural peace, joy, and abundant life God has prepared for you as a woman who seeks to honor and please Christ above everything else in this world. Jesus and the Holy Spirit are the keys here. I can't do the hard work for you, but I am thrilled to have the privilege of walking beside you on this exciting journey. I still have thousands of miles to go myself. None of us will reach total perfection until we are in heaven, face-to-face with Jesus our Lord. There are no guarantees of specific results in your marriage or in your husband's life as you seek to please God, but you are guaranteed that God will radically change *you* when you seek Him with all your heart and desire to walk in full obedience to Him.

"For I know the plans I have for you," declares the Lord, "plans to prosper you and not to harm you, plans to give you hope and a future. Then you will call on me and come and pray to me, and I will listen to you. You will seek me and find me when you seek me with all your heart. I will be found by you," declares the LORD. (Jer. 29:11–14)

"I am the LORD your God,
 who teaches you what is best for you,
 who directs you in the way you should go.
If only you had paid attention to my commands,
 your peace would have been like a river,
 your well-being like the waves of the sea." (Isa. 48:17–18)

Note: If you have very serious problems in your marriage—physical abuse, severe emotional or spiritual abuse, drug or alcohol addictions, uncontrolled mental health disorders, criminal activity, extreme control and manipulation, sexual infidelity, and so on—please find godly, experienced, appropriate help as soon as possible! If you are not safe, please try to get yourself and your children to safety. I do not ever condone abuse or sin against anyone. I don't want wives to sin against husbands and I don't want husbands to sin against wives. Severe marital issues go beyond the scope of this book. I am writing as an older wife, a friend and sister in the Lord, mentoring younger wives about godly marriage. Those with severe problems will need one-on-one help from godly, wise, mature, experienced, licensed professionals and resources geared to the specific issues they are facing.

Introduction

Matthew and Jen

One evening, Matthew decided to grill steaks on the deck for supper. There were lots of flies swarming near the grill, so he asked their teenage son, Jacob, to get the fly swatter. Jen laughed and said, "Son, don't get the flyswatter. That's just crazy. You'll never kill all the flies in the woods with one little flyswatter." Jacob obeyed his mom and went inside, ignoring Matthew's request. Jen was surprised when Matthew suddenly shut down and stayed quiet for the rest of the day. Jen had no idea what her husband was so upset about.

John and Megan

One morning, Megan was getting ready for work and making a special breakfast for John's relatives who were staying at their house for a few days. John entered the kitchen and Megan said, "Honey, can you help me for a minute? I'm trying to finish getting a couple things ready, but I really need to get out the door." John replied, "Don't bother; it's fine." Megan got a bit defensive and said, "Well, I was trying to help you so you knew what you could offer your family for breakfast," and her husband retorted, "They are not babies. They know what they will want to eat—and besides, they aren't *your* family."

Megan glared at John and shot back, "So, you are going to just let them fend for themselves when they wake up?" They continued to throw verbal jabs back and forth at each other for a while until

Megan became exasperated and said, "You are unbelievable!" After more tense interaction, John said harshly, "If you would just shut your mouth, we wouldn't have any of these problems." Megan left for work upset and bewildered about what had just happened. How could an innocent request for John's help to be good hosts for his relatives lead to so much hurt? Why was John being so difficult? The whole day was ruined.

Greg and April

April had to work late, as usual. When she got home, she was glad to smell that a delicious, hot supper was waiting for her. She walked into the kitchen and saw Greg smiling and getting the food on the table. Then she noticed the sink. It was overflowing with dirty pots and pans. Her heart sank. She knew it would be thirty minutes of work for her to hand wash all those dishes, not to mention the time it would take to clean up the grease that had splattered all over the stove and counter-tops. Greg saw April look at the dishes and said proudly, "Look, honey, I rinsed the pots and pans for you!" She sighed in exasperation and gave Greg a very sarcastic lecture. "Yeah. That's just *great!* You get a C+. You still left me a bunch of dirty dishes to wash by hand. Why wouldn't you have washed them yourself instead of leaving them for me to do?" The smile quickly left her husband's face.

What could have been a fun, romantic, beautiful, intimate time ended up being a time of hurt feelings, bitterness, and silence. Greg spent the evening like he usually did—engrossed in the TV and not responding much to his wife. April felt the way she often did: ignored, exhausted, unappreciated, overwhelmed, lonely, resentful, and upset.

What Is Going On Here?

Why is it so difficult to have a simple conversation with our husbands? Why is there so much tension between husbands and wives today? Why do men have to be so stubborn, aggravating, and complicated?

Why can't they just do what we tell them to do and focus on making us happy? Life would be so much easier, right?

It's like there is some huge missing piece of the puzzle in our marriage relationships in recent decades. We know things could be better. We try so hard to improve our marriages on our own. Maybe we even read lots of Christian marriage books and pray daily, but we just can't seem to get our husbands to cooperate. We give our husbands helpful suggestions and wise advice; share our opinions; tell them all the things we are thinking and feeling; and explain how disconnected, unloved, lonely, and hurt we feel in our marriages. We tell them all the things they could do to be better husbands and to make us feel more loved. We tell them they are not paying enough attention to us. We tell them they need to be more plugged in with our children and more romantic with us. We try to be loving and helpful, try to make time to talk and connect with our husbands, and yet many times we don't feel very loved in return. Or maybe we don't share how hurt we are; we just stay shut down, depressed, afraid, and lonely.

Let's get personal here. Are you feeling betrayed that marriage isn't living up to your expectations? Do you cry into your pillow over the lack of romance, connection, and vibrancy in your marriage? Perhaps you're following the Golden Rule—you try to talk with your husband and love him the way you want to be loved in return, but it doesn't seem to work. You are trying to be a good Christian wife but it seems like your husband is just not holding up his end of the deal. You may be *deeply* hurting and wounded in your marriage. You're thinking that if only your husband would change and be more loving, kind, patient, verbal, attentive, romantic, and understanding, the problems in your marriage would all be solved . . .

That's what I used to think! Then, God dramatically opened my eyes. What I was missing is actually something that had been right in front of me in the Bible all of my life. It's just that God's design for marriage has been largely forgotten and so twisted by our culture that I didn't even recognize what God was actually asking me to do as a wife. What He is still asking me to do. And what He asks of all wives.

In Ephesians 5, God gives very explicit commands to husbands and wives and explains His primary purpose and design for marriage. If you are like I was earlier in my marriage, you may have spent more time thinking about how your husband could do a better job obeying God's commands than thinking about what God may desire to change in you. In this book we will examine only what God commands us to do as wives and how that plays out every day in very practical ways that we may never have thought about before. I will not be focusing on what God tells husbands to do here, but that does not mean our husbands are off the hook. All of God's Word still applies to them, just like it does to us. They will answer to God for their own obedience to Him and for being the men He has called them to be. But right now, I would love for us to concentrate on just our relationship to God as women. We have so much power to breathe healing and blessing into our marriages when we choose to live in the center of God's will, His wisdom, His Word, and His Spirit's power. I pray that we might see with fresh eyes what God has to say to us in the Bible as women and wives today.

It is my prayer that in this book we might examine what it actually means to be a godly wife in today's culture. We will explore what disrespect looks like from a husband's perspective. We will look at our own controlling tendencies as daughters of Eve. We will dive into practicalities about how to genuinely respect our husbands, and we will dig into the widely misunderstood concept of biblical submission. We will talk about why God's design works—how it brings freedom, joy, and intimacy with God and our spouses. We will also discuss practical steps for us all to move toward becoming the women God desires us to be. Most of all, we will examine our own intimacy with Christ, our submission to Him as Lord, and our level of reverence for Him.

Our Story

Greg and I met when I was fifteen and he was sixteen, and we dated for six years before getting married. He was my only boyfriend. I did break up with him once for three miserable weeks right before I started college in 1991. Other than that, we had practically zero conflict. We were talking about marriage by the end of my tenth-grade year in high school. I couldn't wait to get married to Greg. He was such a solid, responsible, trustworthy, handsome, intelligent, athletic, high achieving, thoughtful, loving, godly guy. He took all honors classes just like I did. He cared about my feelings and gave thoughtful gifts to my family members every Christmas. He took me out on a date once per week and allowed me to have long, deep discussions with him about all kinds of world problems and theological subjects every night during our hour-long phone conversations. My family loved him and I had my parents' blessing. My marriage to Greg was going to be the best thing ever! All my dreams would come true and we were going to live "happily ever after."

We both were raised in strong Christian homes, both accepted Christ when we were small children, and had parents who are still married (to their first and only spouses). All of our parents have college degrees. They are all believers in Christ. They are all responsible with money. They love their spouses and children dearly. Greg's father is a minister and my father is a deacon. Our parents didn't have big fights. They were not perfect, of course, but there were no major problems, addictions, threats of divorce, affairs, or anything awful in our families of origin. We had pretty good examples of marriage and we were both dearly loved and well cared for as children.

In my mind, Greg and I were totally prepared for marriage. No, we didn't have premarital counseling, but why would we need it? I was going to be "Mrs. Gregory Cassidy." Sigh! I didn't pay much attention to the marriage books I read when they got to chapters on "conflict" because I *knew* we would not have conflict. We wouldn't be like all those other couples. We were going to do the whole marriage thing the *right* way and it wouldn't be difficult whatsoever. We had a storybook Christian romance . . . until we got married. We had done almost everything "right." No one should have been more prepared for marriage than we were, or so I pridefully thought.

Our Launch into Wedded Bliss

I was bursting with happiness on that hot, sunny, summer South Carolina afternoon when we left our wedding reception. The fragrance of warm pine needles was thick in the air and the three stately magnolia trees were in full bloom in the churchyard. My long, thick, wavy brown hair stuck to my neck and back even inside the church. The air conditioning could hardly keep up with all three-hundred-plus people in the building. My cheeks were sore from smiling so much. Everything went perfectly during the ceremony and reception. Finally, we were husband and wife! Greg and I ran together down the concrete front steps of our church as our guests and family pummeled us with birdseed. Then we got in the car to drive away as husband and wife. Happily-ever-after was totally in the bag! We stayed in Pigeon Forge, Tennessee, for our honeymoon in an adorable little condo with our own kitchen. I was ecstatic.

I loved every second of being with my new husband. This is what I had waited for all those six long years and it was glorious! I was excited about everything—going grocery shopping together, watching Greg shave in the mornings, talking for hours on end, and constantly being alone together. I loved the intimacy we shared and was so thankful we had waited to consummate our union on our wedding night. This was heaven. *This* is what I had always dreamed marriage would be. I had never felt so loved, fulfilled, safe, and happy in my life. Everything was absolutely perfect . . . for three short days. Then we came home from our honeymoon, and the challenges and problems began.

> "*This* is what I had always dreamed
> marriage would be. . . . Everything
> was absolutely perfect . . .
> for three short days."

MY SHORT LIST OF UNSPOKEN EXPECTATIONS

While I couldn't have verbalized my expectations at the time, and in retrospect the list was much longer than this, I fully expected:

- Us to spend four to five hours per night together talking, laughing, having a great time connecting, enjoying each other, being alone together, and cuddling*
- Greg's undivided attention just about any time I wanted it
- Daily physical intimacy
- Us to have our own place that was just ours, like "real adults"
- Us to make our decisions completely on our own
- Greg to get a wonderful engineering job immediately
- Us to be totally financially independent

---

*Those of you who are married are probably laughing already.

- Greg to initiate prayer and read the Bible with me daily (even though we hadn't done that when we were dating)
- Us to both be relatively healthy for a long time
- Us to both be happy just about every moment of every day, especially the first few years of our marriage
- Greg to verbally gush loving words over me on a daily basis
- Greg to make me happy and to make me feel loved and cherished
- Greg to feel happy, loved, and cherished by me
- Greg to agree with me and to do basically anything I wanted him to do because we would always agree—his thinking and priorities would always line up with mine
- To never have to forgive anything very significant
- To not have to suffer
- Greg to think, feel, and act exactly like me

My Abrupt Clash with Reality

For the first three months of our marriage, Greg and his dad worked feverishly—six days per week until way after midnight every night, after they worked their full-time day jobs—fixing up an old house for us. One week into our marriage, I severely sprained my lower back as I bent down to paint shelves. (I should have bent from the knees!) Suddenly, I couldn't get out of bed by myself, couldn't put on my own shoes, couldn't help with fixing up the house, sometimes couldn't even walk because my back would often go out. Intimacy became almost impossible for many months. I was consumed by fear, doubt, loneliness, and depression like I had never experienced in all of my twenty-one years. I didn't want to tell my friends or my sister how miserable I was. I did call my mom every day, crying. Other than that, I just stayed in a room by myself in bed alone—in constant and severe physical, emotional, and spiritual pain. I was so afraid I might not ever recover from my back injury. I thought Greg didn't love me because he was spending all his time working or fixing up the house. He seemed to ignore me. He just fell into bed exhausted every night and turned his back to me without a word and without even a kiss while I cried and tried to tell him what I needed. No response. One issue piled on another, and another. I felt unloved, neglected, abandoned, rejected, and ignored. I believed everything my feelings told me without even questioning that there might be another way to look at the situation.

I didn't know how much I misunderstood my loving, young, inexperienced husband that summer and what a difficult time he was having on his end of our marriage. He was trying so hard to make me happy and to provide well for me by fixing up the house. He and his dad were killing themselves trying to get things done on that old house as quickly as possible in the time they had after work. Greg was also having many trials of his own that I didn't appreciate. Of course, now I know that my understanding of his motives toward me was grossly inaccurate, but I didn't know any other way to look at things at the time. I had zero understanding that men and women see the world very, very differently and that the real issue was my misunderstanding, not that Greg didn't love me.

Now I know that my reactions to Greg and to our circumstances made things infinitely more difficult than they already were. Greg did not think, feel, or act like me. He was trying to show his love for me by working on the house to make a beautiful place for me to live with him and by going to work to provide for me. He was trying to find a good job so he could provide more adequately for me. He was trying to be considerate of my fragile back by not touching me so that he didn't hurt me. He was completely exhausted from working forty hours per week at his job, sending out dozens of résumés each week, receiving constant rejection letters from potential employers, and then working forty more hours per week on the house we were going to live in. He didn't know what to do with me and had never seen me so upset. He thought if he respectfully left me alone, I would get better. I didn't get better. He began to shut down. He didn't tell me that the things I did and said hurt him. Instead of me being grateful for all that Greg and his parents were doing for me, appreciating their incredible generosity for helping us with a house, I lashed out at them all in anger and resentment. I had never experienced not having my way before and I did not handle things well at all. It turns out that I was a lot more spoiled and selfish than I ever realized before I got married.

Thankfully, things did get better after those first three months. Eventually, the renovations on the house were finished and, after about eight months, my back got a bit stronger. We had more time together again. Unfortunately, I embraced some toxic lies that first summer, and we set a few very unhealthy patterns in our relationship that impacted our marriage for many years to come.

My Attempts to Fix Things

Even after those first extremely painful three months, it seemed to me that Greg "wouldn't lead" in our marriage. I mean, I would ask him about something and wait for ten to thirty seconds. Sometimes, on my really patient days, I might wait for a few minutes (sighing and rolling my eyes and tapping my fingers impatiently after a minute, of course). When my husband wouldn't make a decision by then, I would just take over and make the decisions myself because I clearly "had to." I thought Greg just wouldn't tell me what he wanted to do. I had no clue that he didn't know what he wanted right away or that he needed more time to make decisions, that this was just part of his personality. Sometimes Greg did make decisions or say what he wanted eventually, but if I didn't agree with him, I made sure to argue for what I thought was right and filibuster my solution until he would agree to do things my way. Greg pulled away more and more and let me make many decisions without any input from him.

I began to think that I was so much more spiritually mature than Greg was. I read my Bible practically every day. I never saw him read his Bible or pray. I prayed for four hours a day sometimes—surely that made me very holy! I prayed and prayed that God would change Greg and make him be the man I thought God wanted him to be. I told God to make Greg be a strong, godly leader and a loving, attentive, affectionate husband. Greg needed to love me like Christ loved the church! Greg needed to stop wasting time on worldly things like TV and focus on the important things in life: God and me. Well, especially *me*. I was convinced that Greg was the problem in our marriage. He became increasingly quiet, passive, and unplugged. He hardly seemed to have opinions anymore. He mostly just watched TV all the time or worked on house projects. Greg had a lot of initiative when we were dating and engaged. Why did he turn into a totally different person after we got married? Funny, he never seemed to appreciate all my helpful suggestions and attention.

"I was convinced that Greg was the problem in our marriage."

My Problem

I was the dominant twin with my sister as we were growing up, so that talkative leadership role just felt normal to me. It was all I knew. I shared *all* my thoughts and feelings with Greg, holding nothing back, just like I had with my sister. When Greg didn't object to what I said, I assumed he agreed with me, just like I had always assumed my sister agreed with me. Turns out that silence doesn't always mean agreement—for sisters or husbands. Sure wish I had learned that a long time ago! Then I became a pharmacist, which probably only increased my tendencies to take over and handle things myself in our marriage, too. Pharmacy also encouraged my obsessive-compulsive and perfectionistic personality traits. When you are a pharmacist, getting things right ninety-nine percent of the time is not good enough. I expected total perfection from myself, from Greg, from everyone. I also didn't realize

I needed to turn off my "patient counseling" mode when I got home. I was used to telling my technicians and patients what to do at the pharmacy. I also told my husband what to do a lot at home. I knew what I wanted and how I was going to get it. I worked hard in school and expected to make all As. I was super-critical of myself and overly responsible, and had little grace for myself or anyone else. Really, I treated Greg pretty much the same way I had always treated myself, only I was probably harder on myself.

I thought I knew best about almost everything: for other people, for my husband, and for myself. Deep down in my soul, I thought I knew better than God, even though I would never have consciously admitted that. I thought people needed my wonderful advice, wisdom, and "help." I was rewarded for all my efforts and my Type A personality in school and in pharmacy with great grades, full scholarships, the praise of all of my teachers, lots of good friends, and customer service awards at work. Why didn't my winning approach work with my husband?

There were so many things about femininity, masculinity, marriage, and the roles of husbands and wives that I just accepted "as is" from our culture and never really questioned. I thought I *was* being a godly wife. I had read God's instructions about marriage many times. I read, "the wife must respect her husband" (Eph. 5:33) and thought, "Check! I do that." I mean, I didn't throw things—well, except for that one time that I threw a pair of panties at Greg that first summer we were married. They didn't even come close to hitting him, and they were clean, so that definitely didn't count as disrespect on my part. I didn't scream, cuss, threaten divorce, hit him, or leave him. I never called him names like "idiot," or, "jerk," or "stupid." I never even used the phrase "shut up." Yes, that first summer, I really *wanted* to hurt Greg physically because I was hurting more than I ever had emotionally and felt very unloved. But I didn't actually hit him. And I was tempted to leave at times, but I didn't actually leave. So, that didn't count as disrespect either. Yes, I raised my voice sometimes but that was only because Greg seemed to ignore me. He had never ignored me before. Surely he would hear and care about my feelings if I upped the volume and demanded that he give me the love, attention, and affection he used to give me so easily before we were married. I was being totally respectful, in my mind. I treated my husband a lot better than many other women treated theirs.

I knew about God's command for wives to "submit yourselves to your own husbands as you do to the Lord" (Eph. 5:22). When my husband would (very rarely) insist on something, I would eventually concede to him, knowing he was supposed to be the leader in our marriage. But my "submission" was only after a lot of me arguing my case, trying to get him to change, explaining how I was right, telling him how my way was much better and more biblical than his, and sharing with him how wrong he was. I was not a cheerful follower. I would grumble, argue, stew, and complain.

I didn't realize what I was doing at the time, but I tried to force Greg to "submit" to me. Truthfully, I expected everyone to not just submit to me, but to agree with me and do things my way. I mean, I was "right." That was obvious. So it was my duty and responsibility to try to change Greg's mind so that he could see things in proper perspective like I did. What could be more important than being right on an issue?

I would try to get Greg to lead sometimes, but only in the way I thought he should. I didn't realize there was any other way to think than my way. I left no room or grace for him to be masculine and to think, feel, and process like a man, or to be himself with his own unique personality. I often felt so lonely in our marriage—stressed, anxious, overwhelmed, and worried. Our marriage was not horrible. It was probably better than most. But, I knew there could be so much more intimacy on every level. I constantly tried to figure out how to make things happen the way I thought they should. I carried the weight of the marriage on my shoulders and felt spiritually, emotionally, and financially responsible for all of the decisions. I never had peace. I didn't realize that if I disrespected my husband's God-given authority over me, trusted myself instead of God, and cherished bitterness and pride in my heart, my prayers weren't going to be heard. My sin poisoned my relationships with God and with Greg. The problem was, I didn't see my sin at all.

Finding the Missing Piece of the Puzzle

We were at our church bookstore in December of 2008 when I picked up a copy of *Love and Respect* by Dr. Emerson Eggerichs. Dr. Eggerichs writes, "Yes, love is vital, especially for the wife, but what we have missed is the husband's need for respect."[1] He said, based on Ephesians 5:22–33, that husbands need respect just as much as wives need love. *What?* I had never heard this concept before. I turned and asked Greg incredulously right there in the aisle of the store, "This book says that husbands need respect as much as wives need love. That can't be right, can it?" My husband rocked my world when he casually said, "Yeah. I'd say that is true," and then turned back to looking at a book he had picked up.

What? The rest of the world froze for me in that bookstore while my understanding of my being a good wife crumbled apart. I had never questioned my assumptions that men and women are emotionally and spiritually identical and that we all have the exact same needs. Suddenly, the history of our entire fourteen-plus years of marriage flashed through my mind. I saw it all from a totally new and unflattering perspective. If my being a godly wife was all about how much I respected Greg, not about how much I loved him, I realized that I was in serious trouble!

God opened my eyes in that moment and proceeded to quietly show me over the next few days as I read that book that *I* had actually been sabotaging and destroying our marriage. I had been hurting Greg deeply. *Me.* That was a shock. I didn't even know Greg was hurting at all because he never said he was upset with me. I learned that Greg was reacting to the way I had treated him to protect himself. That is why he shut down and became so passive. He didn't feel safe with me. He didn't feel respected by me. He had never said a word about any of this. I had assumed that Greg would tell me right away if I ever wounded him. I mean, I was plenty verbal about the times I felt hurt and unloved by him. It was like I was looking at my "godly wife report card" where I had expected to get at least an A if not an A+, and I actually got a D. I was devastated and appalled at myself. Everything suddenly made sense. This was the missing piece of the puzzle of our marriage. If only I had known that first summer we got married that Greg was hurting too, I would have wanted to make things right. I never intended to hurt my husband. How heartbreaking to finally see that I had hurt him unknowingly for so many years.

Greg amazed me. It took him all of two seconds to forgive me for a decade and a half of my disrespect, pride, and control in our marriage. Wow. I realized that there was no way I could have forgiven him that quickly of anything, if I could have ever forgiven him at all. I began to see that Greg had more godly character than I did in some important areas. I told Greg, "One day, when I figure all of this respect stuff out, you are going to feel like the most respected husband on the planet!" He laughed . . . in a good way.

EMBARKING ON A JOURNEY OF CHANGE

My journey of thousands of miles began with a single, excruciatingly painful and humbling step. I seriously wanted to go live by myself in a cave and never speak to another person again. I had no idea before I read Eggerichs's book, and God began to expose the motives of my heart, that almost every motive and thought in my head had been sinful for many years. How did I never see any of this sin before? How could I go forward? I realized I had been disrespectful and controlling to other people in my life, too, and I went to each person to apologize to them for my sin.

I took a few big steps back emotionally from everyone in my life and began to seek God and His truth as I never had before—in total humility and utter desperation. I knew I didn't know how to relate to people or love them God's way without trying to control them. I knew I couldn't speak to Greg or about Greg without being disrespectful. I decided to throw out everything I thought I knew about following Christ, being a woman, being a godly wife, masculinity, and marriage. I began to study and pray for hours every day. I sought to understand and explore my husband's masculine needs. I was amazed to discover how differently my husband looked at life and how differently he thought from me. God gradually opened my eyes to see His design for marriage, godly femininity, and godly masculinity. It was so difficult and frustrating. I had a hard time wrapping my mind around the new things I was learning as I tried to figure out how a godly wife thinks, speaks, and acts in practical ways. It felt like I had to "reinvent the wheel."

> "I decided to throw out everything
> I thought I knew about following
> Christ, being a woman, being a godly
> wife, masculinity, and marriage."

I stopped focusing on my husband's faults and bowed with my face to the floor and begged, "Lord, have mercy on me, a wretched sinner! Change *me!*" I began thanking God and Greg for the good things I could see in Greg. I started a list of things I admired and respected about Greg that I added to daily. I spent much time in confession and repentance of my own sins during my quiet time. I stopped asking God to change Greg. Things slowly started to improve.

I quit running ahead of God and my husband. I decided I would wait right where I was emotionally, spiritually, and geographically until I was eighty years old if I had to, but I was going to wait on God and Greg to lead me. I finally began to understand that God is sovereign, not me. If He wanted me to sit and not go anywhere until my husband led me, then who was I to argue? I would just sit there and waste my life for God, doing "nothing of importance" but obeying Him and living in total obscurity if that was His will. I learned that I did not know best. This whole godly wife thing was all about my walk with Christ; it really wasn't about how Greg treated me. I did not give up my intelligence. But I did give up my worldly wisdom and my sinful self. I made room in my soul for my husband's wisdom and lots of room in my life for God's wisdom. I learned that husbands and God have a much different (usually much longer) timetable from mine, and that is actually a good thing.

Learning a New Language

After a few years of struggle, after reading more than thirty books about godly marriage and godly femininity, after messing up a lot and getting back up and trying some more, and after much earnest and fervent prayer, respect and biblical submission finally began to feel more like "me." It was a lot like learning a new language.

After those first two and a half years, I didn't have to consciously do spiritual and emotional contortion all the time to do the respectful and biblically submissive thing. It began to be more normal as I died to my will, surrendered myself wholly to Jesus Christ, and desired only His glory and His will in my life. I began to truly understand what it meant to follow Jesus as *Lord*. When I started really obeying God, I was shocked at the changes that began to occur in my soul that were unlike anything I had ever experienced. I began bubbling over with joy every day. At first I wasn't sure what the calmness and stillness were in my mind. I didn't know what to think about my sudden lack of anxiety, irritability, loneliness, resentment, bitterness, and worry. It was strange and wonderful! There were all kinds of empty spaces in my head and the constant tight feeling was gone from my chest. Oh! I finally clued in: this is what *peace* feels like! I experienced freedom, stillness, and real peace that lasted days, weeks, and months on end. I savored living in God's power, and I didn't *ever* want to go back to allowing my old sinful flesh to have control. My old thoughts, motives, and words repulsed me now. Living in the power of God's Spirit meant that I got to carry the priceless treasures and riches of heaven around in my soul all the time. Wow. This was the abundant life Jesus described. God's Spirit is really addictive!

> The thief comes only to steal and kill and destroy; I have come that they may have life, and have it to the full. (John 10:10)

I wrote down all of the fears and lies I had been telling myself. I confronted them with the truth of the Bible. I purposely decided to discard the lies I had unknowingly embraced, build my life on God's truth alone, and fully trust Him. If I had everything else I had always wanted but didn't have Jesus, I realized that I would be miserable and nothing could satisfy me. Only Jesus can satisfy the deepest longings of my soul; not my husband, not getting my way, not being in control, not worldly happiness, not romance, not feeling loved by Greg. Control was just an illusion. I didn't have control over much anyway. I began to understand my identity as a woman in Christ. I felt beautiful, feminine (for the first time in my life), empowered, and like I was becoming the woman I had always wanted to be. I finally felt like myself—my *real* self.

I did have to give up my old sinful self. But that was actually not a sacrifice. It was a blessing not to have all that sin in my life destroying my relationship with God, my relationships with others, and me all the time. None of us will achieve sinless perfection on this earth. I realize that I will stumble at times if I am not completely depending on Jesus every moment. These days, I spend time in confession as soon as I notice a tempting thought or recognize a sinful motive beginning to emerge in my heart or if I sin with my words or actions. But Jesus can empower us to walk in victory over sin when His Spirit fills us to overflowing. I have experienced that many times! We don't have to be trapped helplessly in sin and misery all day every day when we have Christ! What great news! He can empower us to grow and mature in our faith over time. Jesus crucified my sinful self and it died with Him on the cross according to Romans 6–8. Then He offered me His new Resurrection Life. Now my old thoughts look like trash next to the beautiful, godly thoughts that Jesus has given me in their place. I also finally began to understand what Greg's needs actually were. It was so exciting to find out I had valuable contributions to make in our marriage that could meet my husband's masculine needs. This was empowering! I wanted to learn and absorb all that I could.

COUNTERINTUITIVE, COUNTERCULTURAL, AND NOT POLITICALLY CORRECT!

You may not respond to God's design for marriage with gut-wrenching sorrow, the way I did. There is a wide range of emotions that women experience when they hear this information for the first time. Some women feel terribly sad. Some feel guilty. Some women feel angry about God's design for marriage when they first hear about it. Often, there is a progression of strong emotions that culminates into a change of heart—then great hopefulness and empowerment. These truths of God's Word can be extremely surprising and difficult to hear after we have been marinating in our ungodly culture and our own sinful thoughts all of our lives. God's ways don't always sound right at first. God's commands for us are counterintuitive, countercultural, not politically correct, and completely against the wisdom of our sinful flesh. The ideas I am going to share with you will, I pray, open your mind to a whole new beautiful world you may have never seen before.

I believe that you owe it to yourself, your husband, and your marriage to at least investigate these different ideas and pray that God might open your eyes to anything He wants you to see. If you're like I was, what you have been doing probably hasn't been working. If that's the case, then what do you really have to lose by doing things God's way? At the very least, we will have a reward in heaven as we walk in obedience to God, whether or not we see results here on earth. And maybe, just maybe, God might work through us to begin to heal our marriages in powerful ways in this life.

> "God's commands for us are
> counterintuitive, countercultural,
> not politically correct, and completely
> against the wisdom of our
> sinful flesh."

Here's a great thing about reading a book. You can close it and go pray and write out your thoughts to God in a journal. You can go cry and repent when God shows you something in your life that He wants you to get rid of. You can read parts again and again if you need to for weeks or months. The key is to take this at the speed that is right for you. You will get the most out of this book if you chew on it slowly and think deeply about yourself and what God is speaking to your heart, allowing Him time and freedom to highlight certain areas for you. You may need to read some parts over and over again to digest them thoroughly in your mind and heart if these are new concepts for you. My purpose is to uphold the Bible as the highest authority and the only source of absolute truth, and to exalt Christ alone. Much of what God's Word says is directly opposed to what our culture, our feelings, and our sinful selves say. It will probably sound foreign. I did things the world's way and my way for a long time, and it did *not* work! I can tell you from my experience and from the hundreds and hundreds of women I have corresponded with online these past few years, God's ways *do* work. I have seen Him transform countless women, men, children, and marriages by His power. Our God knows how to change and heal people who love, trust, and seek to obey Him.

If you are a believer in Christ, my prayer is that this book might be a gateway for you to begin the same journey with God that I began that winter's day in 2008—a journey of learning to abide in Christ and allowing His Spirit to transform you to be more and more like Himself. If you are not yet a believer in Christ, I invite you to begin a relationship with Him today and then begin this journey, too.[2]

Sanctification is the process of dying to self and surrendering completely to Christ as Lord. It is the process of allowing Him to regenerate our souls, to make us into the godly women He wants us to be, to renew our minds, to radically transform us into His likeness, and to make us holy as He is holy. God created us to bring great glory to Himself. That is our primary purpose in this life. For God's glory to shine in my life, I had to dig down and shovel everything out until all I had left was Christ and His Word in my soul. I asked God to rebuild my life on His truth, His Word, and the power of Christ alone.

There are many factors involved in how long this process can take: the examples of our parents; the level of our scars and wounds from our past; how much control we allow the Holy Spirit to have; our willingness to fully repent, submit to, obey, and trust Christ; and the issues our husbands face. You may need an older, godly wife (one who is living in obedience to God in her life and marriage) to mentor you if you are getting stuck. This is a slow process and each wife's and couple's journey is different and will have its own timetable. It is difficult and painful to ask God to show you your own sin and to take a real look at yourself. It's easier to point to your husband's sin and want God to change him. Your greatest power lies in focusing on the things *you* can control and realizing that you cannot change your husband. Really, we can't even change ourselves without God's help. Only God can change people. Thankfully, God can change *us* and make us into His partner in our marriages to bring healing and blessing. Your husband doesn't have to be on board. God is the key. Once you are honoring and obeying God, you stop being a stumbling block to your husband on his journey to hear, know, love, and submit to God.

What I found as I have walked this road is that if I read about what husbands "should do" then I get tripped up. Of course there are things husbands should do and commands God gives to men. Of course there are ways they contribute to the problems in marriage. Men can be too passive or too aggressive just like women can be too passive or too aggressive. Of course husbands are to love their wives as Christ loves the church, and they are to honor and respect their wives in many ways. Thankfully, if in this book I focus only on what God commands for us as wives to do, it detracts nothing from God's commands for our men. His Word for them still stands. Let's trust our husbands to God's sovereignty and to the Holy Spirit's work in their lives. He can open their eyes and show them His truth just fine without us trying to be the Holy Spirit, too.

> "If . . . I focus only on what God commands for us as wives to do, it detracts nothing from God's commands for our men. His Word for them still stands."

Let's stop and pray for you right now, my precious sister in Christ.

Lord,
I don't know the pain and trials this beautiful sister of mine
has endured. I don't know where she is in her walk with You.

But You know her intimately. Let Your Spirit speak to her heart. Help her to embrace You, to desire to trust You, and to fully surrender control to You. I pray that she will lay down all of herself, ready to really hear all that You desire to share with her. I pray for You to empower her to turn away from any lies and sin in her life and to turn to Christ in complete faith, embracing Your life-giving truth. Give her big faith, Lord. I praise and thank You that You are going to make something beautiful from her life for Your greatest glory.

In the name and power of Christ, amen!

Let's Be Honest

There is no way to find real solutions to our marriage problems until we are able to clearly see what we might be contributing to the problem. That is what we are responsible for correcting. I am not saying women are completely responsible for marriage problems. We're not. Neither wives nor husbands are completely responsible for all of the problems in marriages. God's Word says, "for all have sinned and fall short of the glory of God" (Rom. 3:23). That word *all* is pretty inclusive. Every human is sinful in God's sight. Even me. God says that our attempts to be righteous are like "filthy rags" in His sight (Isa. 64:6). The phrase translated "filthy rags" refers to filthy, bloody menstrual rags. That is pretty descriptive of just how worthless my personal attempts at "goodness" and "holiness" are from God's perspective. I need the blood, death, sacrifice, mercy, grace, and forgiveness of Jesus just as desperately as any other human being on the planet! I am not better than anyone else. On my own, there is no good in me. None. I cannot possibly be a godly woman or wife in my own power. In fact, none of us can do this without the power of Christ in our lives. I am extremely aware of this truth every moment of every day. If I begin to hold sin in my heart or allow something else to become more important to me than Christ, I am totally capable of destroying my marriage, my life, and myself. There is never a point at which I no longer must depend completely on the power of God's Spirit. I can mature and grow. And I can have victory over sin as Christ lives in and through me. That is the goal. But I must wait for heaven's gates to be completely perfect and sinless in every way.

This next part (under the heading "A Prayerful Self-Evaluation") can be painful at first—just want to warn you, my precious sister. You may need a box of tissues handy, and you may want to be somewhere by yourself where you can think deeply, and prayerfully allow God to thoroughly inspect your heart. You may even want to begin a prayer journal so that you have space to write out prayers, painful things, concerns, thoughts, struggles, and things God reveals to you. When we come face to face with our own sin, it is not pleasant! But we do need to go through this step to get to the healing steps later.

> *Lord,*
> *I praise You for Your goodness, truthfulness, faithfulness, mercy, grace, forgiveness, justice, holiness, and love. Thank You that nothing in my mind or heart can be hidden from You. Thank You that I am never beyond the reach of Your love. Thank You that there is no sin that is so awful that the blood of Jesus cannot completely pay for it. Help me to recognize and hate sin like You do. Help me to see and receive the love, forgiveness, and abundant new spiritual life You have provided for me through Jesus. Help me to humble myself and put aside any thoughts that I am good in my own power. You alone are good. I need You. Help me to listen to Your still, small voice.*
> *In the name of Christ Jesus, amen.*

God is right here with you, waiting for you to turn to Him in total dependence and trust. You cannot heal yourself, but He knows how to heal you! He has done this millions of times for people just like you and me. He knows exactly what to do. We can count on Him to show us the way.

A Prayerful Self-Evaluation

Part 1. Place a check beside any sentences that apply in your life on at least a monthly basis:

_____ My husband has fallen far short of my expectations that he would make me feel happy and loved.

_____ I want to forgive sometimes, but it just seems impossible.

_____ I talk about my husband in a negative way to other people.

_____ I am primarily concerned with doing things the way I think would be best.

_____ If I feel mistreated, I may scream, cuss, throw things, call names, or say hateful things.

_____ If people upset me, I give them the "cold shoulder" until they apologize to me.

_____ If I feel unloved, I lash out verbally at my husband.

_____ I feel jealous of the good marriages other people seem to have that I don't have.

_____ I look at pornography, read sexy romance novels/erotica, or watch romantic movies often and try to experience real romance and sexual fulfillment through fantasy.

_____ I flirt with other men.

_____ I tell God that my husband needs to change.

_____ I don't think my husband is a good spiritual leader.

_____ I view my husband as being much farther away from God than I am.

_____ If I want something that my husband won't give to me, I demand to have it, I try to make him do what I want, or I sink into a deep, silent depression.

_____ I don't believe I should ever ask my husband to help me.

_____ I don't think I should have needs and desires.

____ I withhold myself sexually from my husband to teach him a
lesson sometimes.

____ I only give myself sexually to my husband when I am in the
mood.

____ I believe that my husband is mostly to blame for the problems
in our marriage.

____ I believe that I am almost always wrong and that I am fully to
blame for the problems in our marriage.

____ I tend to assume the worst about my husband.

____ I believe my husband when he tells me I am a loser.

____ I don't believe my husband's words of love, affirmation,
compliments, and encouragement to me.

____ I can't receive God's love or my husband's love.

____ I try to be prepared for when things go wrong so I can fix
them quickly.

____ I spend large amounts of money without checking with my
husband.

____ I don't really know what I think about a lot of things and just
let my husband handle all of the decisions on his own.

____ It's better if I just stay quiet and don't share my real thoughts
and feelings.

____ I am worried, afraid, and/or anxious a lot.

____ I dress to attract the attention of other men.

____ I believe that I am the spiritually, emotionally, and mentally
mature one in this marriage.

____ I believe that if anything is going to be done "correctly" it is up
to me to handle it.

____ I think about divorce sometimes, or I fantasize about leaving
my husband.

____ I compare my husband to other men.

____ I hate myself.

____ I hate my husband.

____ I am full of guilt and fear.

____ I am so afraid of upsetting my husband.

____ I believe that I am always wrong.

____ I believe that I am always right.

____ I drown my disappointment and pain in alcohol, drugs, shopping, food, cleaning, or perfectionism, or by trying to control things and people around me.

____ I have a lot of anger, resentment, and bitterness toward my husband.

____ I am bitter at God.

Part 2. Place a check beside all of the sentences that generally apply in your life on at least a monthly basis:

____ I am able to respond with God's love even when my husband sins against me, is selfish, or is hateful to me.

____ I have joy in Christ no matter what my husband does or does not do.

____ I may feel sad sometimes or get upset sometimes, but then I take my pain to God and ask Him to help me handle it in a productive way.

____ I have my heart completely set on Jesus. I want Him, His will, and His glory more than anything else in my life.

____ I rarely lose my temper with my husband.

____ I know that I have a valuable role and contribution to make to our marriage and family.

____ I appreciate my husband and am thankful for him.

____ When my husband is having a bad day, I try to think of something I can do to cheer him up.

____ I like blessing my husband.

____ I don't pressure my husband. I give him time to think about things if he needs to.

____ I don't freak out if my husband leaves a mess.

____ I extend grace to my husband freely the way Jesus extends grace to me.

____ If I want or need something, I ask politely with a pleasant tone of voice and a genuine smile.

____ I am careful not to develop close friendships with other men. I guard my heart and my marriage diligently.

____ I don't try to find emotional or sexual fulfillment from movies, romantic novels, or pornography.

____ If my husband responds to me harshly, I usually answer gently.

____ If my husband were to be abusive to me, I know that I would respond with respect for myself, for him, and for our marriage by setting healthy limits and boundaries until he got the help he needed and changed his attitude and behavior toward me.

____ If my husband were to mess up, I trust God to work things out for my ultimate good and His glory.

____ If my husband upsets me, I assume that I may have misunderstood him and don't immediately get angry. I ask some questions to clarify.

____ I am not usually afraid no matter what happens. Ultimately, my faith is primarily in God, not my husband.

____ I trust most of my husband's decisions and cooperate with him often, even when I don't agree with him, unless he is asking me to blatantly sin or do something really dangerous, or he is clearly not in his right mind.

____ I strive to have a spirit of saying yes to things that are important to my husband.

____ What my husband wants is important to me, but what God wants is most important to me.

____ I am trustworthy and have nothing to hide from my husband.

____ I consciously work to do good for my husband no matter what happens.

____ I cooperate with my husband about our spending and budget.

_____ I give myself freely and joyfully to my husband sexually whenever possible (unless he is involved in adultery or there are major reasons why I cannot make myself available to him).

_____ I watch my words, my tone of voice, my facial expressions, and my actions to be sure that I bless my husband.

_____ I show honor to my husband and to Christ in the way that I dress and act.

_____ I don't call my husband names.

_____ I depend on God to meet most of my emotional and spiritual needs, not my husband.

_____ I think of my husband as my friend.

A Look at the Results

If you checked any of the items in Part 1, this book is for you! I can sure relate to you. I could not have checked many of the items in Part 2 for the vast majority of my marriage. That is because *self* was squarely in control back then, even though I thought I was an amazing Christian. I had no idea how to have a Spirit-filled life. This is not about me trying harder or me being perfect. Becoming a godly wife is not about following a bunch of rules. Those things are impossible! This is about learning to allow God's Spirit to work through my life as I seek to live for Him. His ways are not oppressive. If I am feeling overwhelmed and overburdened, I am probably trying to do this in my power, apart from the Spirit's strength.

> "Becoming a godly wife is not about following a bunch of rules. . . . If I am feeling overwhelmed and overburdened, I am probably trying to do this in my power, apart from the Spirit's strength."

Take my yoke upon you and learn from me, for I am gentle and
humble in heart, and you will find rest for your souls. For my
yoke is easy and my burden is light. (Matt. 11:29–30)

God is about to do some amazing things in your life if you are willing to trust Him! It is going to feel very strange and foreign at first, but
what He wants to do is more than worth it! If you only checked items in
Part 2, God is obviously very much at work in your life and His Spirit
is in control much of the time. That is wonderful! I pray that this book
might give you helpful reminders about how to honor your husband
and help you to fine-tune some areas so that faith in Christ and your
marriage might be all that God created them to be. Perhaps God might
even nudge you to consider mentoring some younger wives you know.

By the way, these statements are loosely based on Galatians 5:19–23.
Part 1 shows what I am like as a wife when my sinful nature has control
in my life. Part 2 is what I am like as a wife when God's Spirit has control in my life. Once I experienced God's Spirit being in control, I have
never wanted to go back to doing things my old way!

An Assessment of Your Husband

It is easy for us to think that men are too big and strong to be hurt
emotionally. Or we may think that because men often don't verbalize
their emotions, they don't have feelings. The truth is we have more
power to hurt them than anyone else in their lives, and we may not
even realize what we are doing. My husband, Greg, never said a word
about the pain he experienced in our marriage. He never told me I was
being disrespectful. He never said he was not happy in the marriage.
He never confronted me about my sin. Was I ever shocked to find out
that he did have feelings and that I had deeply wounded him daily for
years. How awful! I want our husbands to feel safe to tell us when we
hurt or upset them just as much as I want us to feel safe to share when
we are feeling hurt or upset. Sometimes husbands do try to tell us that

they are upset or feeling disrespected (which means they feel unloved), but we sometimes don't hear what they are saying.

Now, checkmark each of the following comments you have heard your husband say to you:

____ "I am a grown man. Stop treating me like a child!"
____ "You worry over *everything.*"
____ "You never believe me when I tell you things."
____ "Have a little faith in me."
____ "I can't win here."
____ "I'm not a mind reader."
____ "Trust me."
____ "I told you I would take care of it."
____ "My opinion doesn't even matter around here."
____ "You care more about _____ than you do about me!"
____ "You're smothering me."
____ "Just let me figure it out."
____ "No man could love you like you want to be loved. Not even Jesus!"
____ "Why can't you just be happy?"
____ "How can I lead if you won't follow?"
____ "Why don't you ever have an opinion?"
____ "You expect me to be like your dad instead of being myself."
____ "I don't want to be the only one involved in making this decision."

Some other signs to watch for that probably signal that your husband is feeling disrespected (some of these things can be signs of other significant issues, as well, of course):

- He clenches his jaw.
- He has a hurt expression on his face.

- His countenance falls.
- He shuts down verbally.
- He leaves the room suddenly for "no reason."
- He gets angry "out of nowhere."
- He becomes very emotionally distant.
- He begins spending a lot more time away from home.
- He pulls away sexually and doesn't respond to your advances anymore.

If you are seeing signs that your husband is feeling disrespected by you, prayerfully consider whether you should have a conversation together on this topic. Maybe it's time to say, "Babe, do you generally feel respected by me or do you sometimes feel disrespected? If there are things I am doing that make you feel disrespected, I really want to know about them so that I can work on them. I never want you to feel insulted or disrespected by me." (Of course, if he shares things at this point, be sure to receive them without defending yourself. Just listen and take the issues he talks about to God in prayer.) If you don't believe that God would have you address this verbally yet, it could be that you can just be on the lookout for some of these signals and then when you see any of them, maybe you could say, "Did I come across disrespectfully just now, honey?"

If I argue with my husband that he shouldn't feel disrespected or that he doesn't deserve respect, things will be much worse. I sure wouldn't like it if I felt unloved and my husband said, "You shouldn't feel unloved." Or even worse, "You don't deserve my love." Ouch! God commands a wife to respect her husband without condition or qualification, even if she doesn't think he deserves it, just as He commands a husband to love his wife unconditionally, even if he doesn't think she deserves it (Eph. 5:25–33). God's Word simply says, "The wife must respect her husband." We don't have to respect sin, but our husbands need our genuine respect for them as men just as much as we need their genuine love for us. There is seriously almost nothing more damaging a wife could say to her man than, "You don't deserve my respect!" Men do have feelings. They can hurt, and they can hurt deeply in response to our cutting, disrespectful comments. They may not say anything about it. Ever. Or they may react in anger. But they can be deeply wounded by our careless words. Once you begin to recognize disrespect and how men react, you will quickly realize that it is everywhere. There is a famine of respect for men, husbands, and fathers in our culture. Disrespect for men has become mainstream, unfortunately. It's time to make some serious changes if we expect our marriages and families to thrive, grow, and honor God.

> "If I argue with my husband
> that he shouldn't feel disrespected
> or that he doesn't deserve respect,
> things will be much worse. I sure
> wouldn't like it if I felt unloved and
> my husband said, 'You shouldn't
> feel unloved.' Or even worse,
> 'You don't deserve my love.'"

THE CAUSES OF THE MARITAL POWER STRUGGLE

A number of factors contribute to the "battle of the sexes" in marriage. When our sinful flesh is in control, we bring a lot of destructive power into our relationships. Apart from Christ, this is the only way we can think, speak, and act. The sinful nature cannot create harmony, peace, joy, safety, wholeness, and healthy relationships. Sin always hurts us, others, and God. Marriage is one of the places where sin can cause more pain than it does in almost any other relationship.

1. The Fact That We Are Daughters of Eve

Ever since Adam and Eve fell into sin in the garden of Eden, there has been a power struggle in marriage. Sin brought division, contention, strife, selfishness, and a desire for control to our hearts. Before the fall, Adam held a position of headship in that joyous marriage and Eve was the helpmeet.[1] Adam was the first one created. God gave the command about not eating from the Tree of the Knowledge of Good and Evil to Adam so that Adam could tell Eve later. Adam named Eve because, in creating Adam first, God gave him the position of authority. When they did sin, God spoke to Adam first as the head of his home. Eve was also accountable to God for her sin, of course. Because of sin, both husband and wife were cursed in ways that were unique to their masculinity or femininity. As part of the curse on women, in addition to increased pain in childbirth, God told Eve that she would desire to control her husband. "Your desire will be for your husband, and he will rule over you" (Gen. 3:16). The word for "desire" is the same word that God used when He later addressed Cain—it is a desire to control: "But if you do not do what is right, sin is crouching at your door; it desires to have you, but you must rule over it" (Gen. 4:7).

2. Fear

Fear is a major part of our motivation to grab for control as women. We are afraid we won't be loved, won't be secure, or won't have what we need. We are afraid that we might be rejected, that we might not be lovable, or that we aren't good enough. We are afraid that we aren't beautiful enough or woman enough. We are afraid that we might not be our husbands' first priority the way we want to be. We are afraid of tragedy and loss. We are afraid that we won't have the things, people, and intimacy we want most, so we try to force our way to ensure we are guaranteed to win, not realizing that our fear will cause us to repel the very intimacy we most desire. Like Eve, we may simply fear that we're missing out on something better than what God has given to us. It is only as we are closer and closer to God that His perfect love casts out all fear (1 John 4:18).

The root of these fears will be different for different women. If we didn't feel safe as children, we may have developed a warped, small, wimpy picture of God. Even as adults, if those who were in authority over us did not or could not protect us, or if they abused their authority, we may have come to believe that we can't trust or depend on others and that we need to protect ourselves and cause things to work out right ourselves. If your fear is excessive and you think that is what's behind your motivation to control, you may need to find a godly counselor to help you find peace.

3. Pride

If I have self on the throne of my life instead of God, I probably won't consciously or audibly say, "I am god. Bow down to me." But I will live as if I am in charge, as if I am very powerful, as if I know best, as if I have tons of wisdom, as if I am in control over my life and other people's lives around me, and as if I am sovereign rather than God. If I set myself up as god in my life, then it is my duty and responsibility to make sure that things work out properly according to what I believe is best. I, then, have the right and even the obligation to tell people and God to do things my way.

Of course, in reality, I am not God. I do not have all wisdom. I am not sovereign. I do not have control over much. I do not have the right to expect everyone, including God, to submit to me. When I believe I am totally responsible for people and circumstances in my life to turn out right, and I attempt to take on the weight of God's sovereignty that I cannot possibly carry, I will have incredible anxiety, stress, worry, and fear. I can't have peace. It's impossible for me to experience the filling of God's Spirit in my life while living my own way rather than God's way. He only grants His peace, His joy, and the blessings of the fruit of His Spirit to those who humble themselves before Him, repent of their sins, put all their trust in Him, fully submit to Him, and determine to walk in obedience to His Word through the power of His Spirit living in them. Thankfully, no matter what background, baggage, or sin history we have, with God *all* things are possible! No matter why we learned to do things out of fear or guilt, God calls us to receive His love and healing now and to learn to do things purely out of love for Him as He radically transforms our hearts, minds, and souls.

4. Feelings

Negative feelings can be important indicators that something might be wrong. They are a flag to me that I need to do some journaling and soul searching. Sometimes we make the mistake of always believing our feelings, even when our feelings may not be telling us the truth:

- If I don't feel connected to my husband, then we are not connected.
- If I don't feel loved in this moment, then I am not loved.
- If I feel lonely, then I am alone.
- If I feel afraid, then my fear must be justifiable and unavoidable.

Feelings can be useful indicators, but they are not the source of absolute truth. God's Word is the only reliable source of absolute truth. I must compare my thoughts and the messages of my feelings with the Bible. If I realize I am hormonal with PMS, I purposely ignore my feelings for a day or two and trust Greg's perspective and the truth of God's Word rather than my emotions, because I know that if I trust my feelings at that time, I will crash and burn. There are times when I can trust some of my feelings, but I need to carefully evaluate negative emotions to determine their source. Am I being sinned against? Is there a sinful motive in my own heart? Or am I just exhausted, sick, hungry, or hormonal? If my feelings are accurate, then I can prayerfully consider how God might want me to respond to a difficult situation. If my feelings are not accurate or are of sinful origin, then I can choose to override them rather than being compelled to act on them, which would be destructive. How I thank and praise God that I no longer have to be a slave to my strong emotions!

5. Assumptions and Expectations

When we assume that our husbands or our marriages will be a certain way and we do not get what we expected to, we will probably be upset. We tend to make assumptions about what a good husband is supposed to do, and to expect our husbands to magically meet all of our expectations. You may expect your husband to make up for the things you were lacking as a child or in an abusive relationship in the past, and to heal all of your wounds. You may expect your husband to be just like your father. You may expect your husband to be totally responsible for your happiness or contentment rather than being responsible for your own spiritual growth and your own emotions. You may unwittingly make your husband more important than God in your heart, if you lay the expectation on him that he should meet spiritual and emotional needs for you that really only Jesus Christ Himself can meet.

> "You may unwittingly make your husband more important than God in your heart, if you lay the expectation on him that he should meet spiritual and emotional needs for you that really only Jesus Christ Himself can meet."

A very helpful exercise may be to write down all of the expectations and assumptions you have for your husband and marriage in a journal. Then carefully evaluate your ideas. Many times, the most healthy thing we can do is to lay down our expectations before God and choose to hold our expectations of our husbands very loosely as we purposely seek to find our contentment in Christ alone. It can feel scary to lay down our expectations of our husbands, but as we learn to find contentment in Jesus and nothing else, there is so much freedom, joy, and peace. We can choose to accept our husbands as they are and release them and ourselves from the prison of all of our assumptions and expectations.

THE RESULTS OF THE MARITAL POWER STRUGGLE

When I love with a lot of expectations of what I want to receive in return, I am loving with strings attached. This is not real love, but rather, manipulation:

> "I will love him so that he will love me."
> "I will be kind to him so that he will be kind to me."
> "I will do things for him and give him things so that he will take care of me the way I want him to."

Then we may reason, "If he does not love me the way I want him to, I am totally justified to be hateful to him, to disrespect him, and to hurt him. He didn't meet my expectations, so I can be mean to him and it's okay."

As I try to control my husband, either he will fight me or he will shut me out of his heart. Men do not respond well to being disrespected, smothered, or controlled. When I see his seeming lack of love, my motives become increasingly fear driven. I sabotage our intimacy. I emasculate him. I disrespect him. I wound him. I repel him. I smother him. I try to pressure and force him to do what I want him to do. I become increasingly desperate, needy, and clingy. I am insatiable. No matter what he does at this point, I will not be satisfied. Eventually, my husband realizes he can't meet my needs, please me, or satisfy me, and he gives up even trying. It is not worth his time because I am going to treat him with contempt no matter how hard he tries. He can never measure up and he can never be perfect in my eyes.

Most husbands really want their wives to be happy. I have heard from countless husbands who say they would gladly do almost anything to contribute to their wives' happiness, *if* they believe it is possible for their wives to be pleased and if what the wives desire lines up with God's will. If all my husband sees is my constant unhappiness, contempt, criticism, or condemnation, he loses his motivation to even try to delight me. He may feel totally defeated.

My motives when I am operating out of fear, guilt, or pride are not to love my husband selflessly with the unconditional love of Christ, to bless him, and to honor God. My motives are to try to make him give me what I want from him. My motives are selfish. This is not God's brand of *agape* love that He wants us to have for other believers as described in 1 Corinthians 13:4–8. This is worldly, carnal, sinful "love."

WHO IS IN CONTROL?

Here is one very critical piece of information for us to understand: we don't actually have control over much in this life. We can't control other people. It is not our right or responsibility to control others. If I try to make myself responsible for other people and make them be responsible for me, that is often called being "enmeshed" or "codependent," and it is a destructive mentality. God gave each person a free will and it is not our place to take that away from a grown adult. Healthy relationships involve appropriate boundaries and a proper amount of space spiritually, emotionally, and physically. Each person is responsible for his or her own sin, obedience to God, emotions, and decisions. I can only really control myself, but even then, God's Spirit must be in charge, not me.

"Healthy relationships involve appropriate boundaries and a proper amount of space spiritually, emotionally, and physically."

The mind governed by the flesh is death, but the mind governed by the Spirit is life and peace. (Rom. 8:6)

I have two choices about control in my life:

1. I can allow my sinful flesh to have control. The results are always predictable. If I have *any* sinful behaviors in my life (Gal. 5:19–21), my flesh is in control at that time.
2. I can allow the Spirit of God to have control. When God's Spirit is in control of my life, I will have all of the fruit of the Spirit in increasing measure as God transforms me to be more like Jesus. As I know God, His character, and His truth in greater depth, I begin to understand His sovereignty, and my faith grows. Then I realize I have nothing to fear (1 John 4:18). I experience fruit— abundant supernatural love, joy, peace, patience, kindness, goodness, faithfulness, gentleness, and self-control (Gal. 5:22–23).

I personally had to write out all of the beliefs I held about God, my marriage, my husband, and myself, and compare what I was thinking to Scripture. In my list I found wrong self-talk and ungodly "fixed beliefs"—things I had repeated so often to myself that I believed them to be absolute truth. I studied the Bible to see what it said about these. Discovering and internalizing the truths of Scripture were the keys to transforming my faulty fixed beliefs to align with God's beautiful truths.

I asked God to help me understand and apply His truth and to understand His character. I asked Him to show me my errors and the lies I had believed, as well as sinful attitudes in my heart. I needed Him to expose my warped thinking and every ungodly thing in my heart. I needed to see that everything belonging to my old sinful self was crucified in Christ on the cross and buried with Him. That is past history to God. I received His new life when Jesus was raised from the dead, and now His Spirit lives in me and through me. This journey is not about what I have done or my goodness. I don't have any goodness in me apart from God, according to His Word (Ps. 16:2; Rom. 3:23). This is all about the work Jesus has already finished on the cross and in His resurrection.

You can embark on a similar journey as you begin to examine your own heart and align it to the truths found in Scripture.

Examine your heart.

I think it would be fantastic to write out on the left side of a journal notebook page the things you tell yourself when you are afraid, worried, or upset. That may include things like:

- No one likes me.
- God can't love me.
- I am unlovable.
- I am worthless.
- I am an inconvenience and a burden to everyone.
- I don't have any friends.
- My husband doesn't love me.
- I must have my husband's approval above all else, all of the time.
- ✓ I'm not my husband's biggest priority.
- If my husband loved me, he would . . .
- God owes me . . .
- God is not good.
- People need to just do what I say and everything would be fine!
- God is out to get me.
- I can't trust God.
- I am unattractive.
- My feelings are truth.
- My wisdom is greater than God's wisdom.
- I can trust myself more than I can trust God or His Word.
- If I trust God, He might take away the things and people I love the most.

Search Scripture.

In the list you just wrote, you're likely seeing some of your own faulty fixed beliefs. Now is a great time to combat those with God's truths. If you realize you are telling yourself that you are unloved, for example, search in the Bible for verses about God's love for you. Then write those verses down on the right side of your journal page so that you can fill your mind with God's healing truth.

You may discover Isaiah 49:15, John 3:16, Romans 8:35–39, 1 John 4:19, and many more verses that help you understand that God loves you. This is the truth. You are most dearly loved and cherished by God. God loves you because that is who He is. None of us deserves His love. Yet in His grace, He lavishes His love on us through Christ. Now you can recognize the voice of the enemy when he tempts you to think that you are not loved. You can throw away the lie and meditate on God's truth.

You can search other topics about the other thoughts you have been replaying in your mind as well, and write down God's truth about those things. I like to use online resources like http://www.openbible.info or http://www.biblegateway.com. You can type in a topic and find related verses instantly. Or you can use a concordance.

Then, consciously reject the old, untruthful ways of thinking every time those thoughts flash in your mind, and choose to embrace God's truth and wisdom. I recommend committing some verses to memory that are particularly helpful in combating the lies you have believed in the past. This is how "We demolish arguments and every pretension that sets itself up against the knowledge of God, and we take captive every thought to make it obedient to Christ" (2 Cor. 10:5).

"Consciously reject the old, untruthful ways of thinking every time those thoughts flash in your mind, and choose to embrace God's truth and wisdom."

Talk to God.

Cry out to God; ask Him to help you examine all of your motives, thoughts, and priorities. Probe as deeply as possible into that upon which you have built your faith and life. Don't do this in a hasty, rushed way. Make it part of your quiet time to carefully examine, evaluate, and weigh your thoughts and feelings against Scripture. Allow any negative feelings or emotions to be flags that it may be a good time to do this deep soul-searching again. Some questions to ask yourself:

- In what areas of my life do I not trust God fully?
- Is there anything that is more important to me right now than Jesus?
- What are my greatest fears?
- What do I tell myself about these fears?
- What do I worry about?
- Why do I worry?
- What do I believe I have to have to be content?
- Why do I want this particular thing so much? Is it to please, love, and honor God or to love and bless someone, or is there a wrong motive?

We will continue this daily probing search into our motives, looking for any sin and repenting of it for the rest of our lives, as believers in Christ. Sometimes God reveals layers of sin, fear, unbelief, or warped views over time. Until we really carefully dissect each thought and our true motives under the light of God's Word by the power of His Spirit working in us, we can so easily deceive ourselves and believe that our motives are good when they are actually completely wrong. "The heart is deceitful above all things and beyond cure. Who can understand it?" (Jer. 17:9). The way that we can overcome fear is to know God more through Jesus as He reveals Himself to us in the Bible and to completely submit ourselves to the lordship of Christ. The more we understand

God's true nature and character, the more He fills up all of our vision, and the more our fears and problems shrink and melt away. We don't talk a lot today about consecrating ourselves to God, devoting ourselves wholeheartedly to Christ, or submitting ourselves completely to Christ, but this is exactly what we must do if we are to be free from the fear and lies that have imprisoned us.

Luke 2:11

4

The Absolute Lordship of Christ

Jesus came to be not just our Savior but also our Lord. In fact, He calls everyone who desires to follow Him to deny ourselves, take up our cross, and follow Him. What He asks from us is absolutely everything. But He gave all of Himself for us first. As we begin to understand who God is and how worthy He is of our devotion and obedience, we realize that what Jesus asks us to give up is actually not a sacrifice. It seems like a great burden to us to surrender everything to Christ at first, but He repays us with spiritual blessings that we cannot begin to fathom in this life, and heaven with Him forever when this lifetime is over. When we are in the center of His will, we find the greatest peace, fulfillment, and joy.

UNDERSTANDING GOD'S CHARACTER

God is good.

There is nothing bad in God at all. Everything He makes is good. His desires are good. All of His actions and decisions are good. He is the very definition and foundation of what it means to be "good." He cannot even think one bad or evil thought.

No one is good—except God alone. (Luke 18:19)

At this, Job got up and tore his robe and shaved his head. Then he fell to the ground in worship and said:
"Naked I came from my mother's womb,
    and naked I will depart.
The LORD gave and the LORD has taken away;
    may the name of the LORD be praised."
In all this, Job did not sin by charging God with wrongdoing.
(Job 1:20–22)

God is just.

God is always absolutely just, as much as He is always love. He cannot ignore evil. Someone must pay for every sin and the price is blood—Jesus's blood or the guilty person's blood.

Without the shedding of blood there is no forgiveness. (Heb. 9:22)

The LORD is known by his acts of justice; the wicked are ensnared by the work of their hands. (Ps. 9:16)

God shows wrath toward sin.

God vows that He will pour out His holy anger on those who disobey Him and who do wrong. Many times God gives us years, even decades, to turn from sin and turn to Him in repentance, but if people refuse to turn to God and continue to do evil, He will eventually punish their sin. God is slow to anger, but that does not mean He never has anger. But when He does have anger, it is righteous anger.

In furious anger and in great wrath the LORD uprooted them from their land and thrust them into another land, as it is now. (Deut. 29:28)

God's wisdom is infinitely higher than our own.

God has great wisdom. I do not. I must humble myself and repent of any prideful attitude that I think I have more wisdom than God before I approach His throne.

> Woe to those who quarrel with their Maker . . . Does the clay say to the potter, "What are you making?" Does your work say, "The potter has no hands"? . . . This is what the LORD says—the Holy One of Israel, and its Maker: "Concerning things to come, do you question me about my children, or give me orders about the work of my hands?" (Isa. 45:9–11)

God is holy and is incapable of sin.

God is always perfect. He always does and thinks what is right.

> When tempted, no one should say, "God is tempting me." For God cannot be tempted by evil, nor does he tempt anyone; but each person is tempted when they are dragged away by their own evil desire and enticed. Then, after desire has conceived, it gives birth to sin; and sin, when it is full-grown, gives birth to death. (James 1:13–15)

God is love.

He cannot have unloving motives toward anyone. God's kind of love is defined in 1 Corinthians 13:4–8. His love is displayed in His willingness to send His only Son to die in our place on the cross. The cross most vividly demonstrates how the wisdom, the love, the wrath, the justice, and the holiness of God all work together in harmony. God's wrath was fully satisfied when He poured it out on His Son, Jesus. Then there was justice—sin was adequately paid for in God's holy sight. What good news for us! We don't have to receive God's wrath, but we can receive His gift of love, mercy, and grace instead!

> For God so loved the world that he gave his one and only Son,
> that whoever believes in him shall not perish but have eternal
> life. For God did not send his Son into the world to condemn
> the world, but to save the world through him. (John 3:16–17)

God is sovereign.

Every book of the Bible points to God's sovereignty. He is able to use
even demons, sin, Satan, evil, and sinners to ultimately accomplish His
purposes even though He does not cause evil. He has the power to limit
evil and to define the parameters and scope of evil. He is sovereign over
evil and yet separate from it. He has the power to use what sinful people
intend for evil to accomplish good. There is nothing in the universe
that is outside of God's control. Our free will and God's sovereignty
coexist somehow without conflict in a mysterious way that we cannot
begin to fathom. We are responsible for our actions. We make our own
choices. We face consequences for our choices. At the same time, God
is in control and uses all things for His purposes, as the story of Joseph
and his brothers demonstrates when Joseph forgives his brothers four-
teen years or so after they sold him into slavery.

> But Joseph said to them, "Don't be afraid. Am I in the place of
> God? You intended to harm me, but God intended it for good
> to accomplish what is now being done, the saving of many
> lives. So then, don't be afraid. I will provide for you and your
> children." And he reassured them and spoke kindly to them.
> (Gen. 50:19–21)

God is also merciful, all-powerful, all-knowing, never-changing,
and patient. He exists outside of time and space. He is the Creator of
the universe. He is perfect, faithful, true, and right. He keeps all of His
promises. He cannot lie. He is the only God there ever was or ever will
be. He is worthy of all of our worship, praise, adoration, and obedience.

I think a fantastic idea for Bible study would be to pull up a Bible website online (like http://www.openbible.info) and research the character of God or the attributes of God. The more we understand who God really is, the easier it is to trust Him and put our faith in Him. He doesn't expect us to put our faith in Him without any evidence of His existence or without an understanding of who He is. We can know Him as He presents Himself to us accurately in His Word.

UNDERSTANDING MY CHARACTER

I would sin against any man I marry. Any man I marry would wrong me at times. Some worse than others, true. But all spouses sin against each other. I don't buy our culture's concept of a "perfect soul-mate" who meets all of our needs without fail. Loving a sinner is painful; even forgiven sinners who have Christ as Lord stumble into sin at times or unintentionally hurt others. Love involves great cost and sacrifice. Look at how much it cost Jesus to love us. Marriage gives us a taste of the deep love and pain God experiences in His relationship with us. People have free will. They can choose to do wrong against God and against others.

> "Marriage gives us a taste of the deep love and pain God experiences in His relationship with us."

Here is something shocking that God showed me as I began to learn about becoming a godly wife: *my level of respect and biblical submission toward my husband is a direct indication of my level of reverence for and submission to Jesus Christ.* If I am disrespectful toward my husband and I try to control him and our marriage, I would be the same way no matter what my husband does or who my husband is. My respect or disrespect comes out of *my* heart and soul. It is about my character and it has almost nothing to do with what my husband does or does not do. God counts the way I treat others, including my husband, as how I treat Him (Matt. 25:40). It is easy to assume that if I had a more loving husband, I would be a better wife. But God showed me that the kind of wife I am and how I respond to my husband (and others) is all about my character and whether my sinful old self is in control or not. My husband can make it easier or harder for me to respect him, of course, just like I can make it harder or easier for him to love me. The specific things I choose to respect about my husband have to do with his character. But my level of respect and whether I respect my husband or not is about my obedience to God's Word and my relationship with Christ. The question is not, "Does my husband deserve my respect and my biblical submission in my opinion?" The real question is, "Does Jesus deserve my respect and submission?"

> "My respect or disrespect comes
> out of *my* heart and soul. It is
> about my character and it has
> almost nothing to do with what my
> husband does or does not do."

In Ephesians 5:22–23, God gives commands to me as a wife, not suggestions. As Christian women, we say we want God's will. This is it, in black and white. The world says, "Respect must be earned." I agree that in the world, such as in business, this is true to some degree. However, believers in Christ are to treat all people with honor and respect. Marriage is not a business contract and it is not of this world. It is a sacred covenant designed by God before the fall to represent the profound mystery of the relationship between Jesus Christ and His church. The husband is to portray the sacrificial, humble, selfless, wise, servant-hearted, unfailing love of Jesus for His church, where Jesus is the Head of the body of Christ. The wife is to portray the reverence, adoration, and submission of the church to Jesus (Eph. 5:22–33). Glad, intelligent, willing submission responding to kind, humble, powerful, selfless love. What a beautiful picture!

Focusing on My Submission to Christ

My job is to uphold my end of the marriage covenant through the power of God's Spirit working in me. I am responsible to God to accurately portray my part in this "play." My husband is responsible to God for correctly portraying his part. God will grade us each separately when we stand before Him in heaven one day. If my husband sins against me, God does not give me a free pass to sin against him, even though it may be very tempting for me to do so. The same is true for my husband—he gets no free pass to sin against me either.

Some of God's purposes in marriage are to bring glory to Himself, to make us holy, to provide godly environments and examples for our children to emulate, and to display tangible flesh-and-blood examples of His loving relationship with His people. He wants to use our marriages to bring many to Christ!

Now, rather than "looking out for number one," I present myself daily as a living sacrifice for Christ, taking up my "cross" and dying to self (Luke 9:23–24; Rom. 6:11; Gal. 5:13–26). I humble myself before God and others, taking on the heart of a servant. I become a slave of Christ Jesus instead of being a slave to sin like I was. I don't focus on making sure my needs are met first. My needs are important. I can ask for what I need. My husband's needs are important and he can ask for what he needs. God is much more important than anyone or anything and He is able to abundantly meet my needs. I adopt the mind, heart, and Spirit of Christ. Now I look out for the needs of others first (like my husband). I do this from a place of great strength and power in Christ, not in the weakness of my flesh. I am not a doormat. I am not a mindless robot or a subhuman "slave" without desires, ideas, and opinions.

My goal is not ultimately to please my husband. I am not making my husband my god. That would be disastrous! My goal is to bring great joy to my Lord Jesus.

> "My goal is not ultimately to please
> my husband. . . . My goal is to
> bring great joy to my Lord Jesus."

Jesus changes my nature and desires to match His own as I cooperate with Him. I no longer desire to repay evil with evil, but I long to repay evil with good because that is what pleases God (Rom. 12:9–21). I want to speak the truth in love (Eph. 4:15). I don't want to deceive people or act like I'm fine if I actually have a problem. I desire to be honest, authentic, vulnerable, direct, respectful, kind, humble, gentle, patient, and loving (by God's definition in 1 Cor. 13:4–8) and to have self-control through Christ. I long to be sensitive to God's Spirit to know when it is better to extend grace and not bring up a matter or when it is important to speak up gently, truthfully, courageously, boldly, respectfully, and lovingly. I know I need God's wisdom to know what to do in each situation. I see that holding grudges is a toxic, sinful way to live that imprisons me. I long to forgive freely so that God will forgive me (Matt. 6:14–15). Instead of doing marriage my way or the culture's way, I submit myself to Christ and am willing to obey Him and do everything His way—even if it is unpopular or weird, or if others hate me for it.

> Submit yourselves, then, to God. Resist the devil, and he will flee from you. Come near to God and he will come near to you. Wash your hands, you sinners, and purify your hearts, you double-minded. Grieve, mourn and wail. Change your laughter to mourning and your joy to gloom. Humble yourselves before the Lord, and he will lift you up. (James 4:7–10)

Therefore, I urge you, brothers and sisters, in view of God's mercy, to offer your bodies as a living sacrifice, holy and pleasing to God—this is your true and proper worship. Do not conform to the pattern of this world, but be transformed by the renewing of your mind. Then you will be able to test and approve what God's will is—his good, pleasing and perfect will. (Rom. 12:1–2)

Anyone who loves their father or mother more than me is not worthy of me; anyone who loves their son or daughter more than me is not worthy of me. Whoever does not take up their cross and follow me is not worthy of me. Whoever finds their life will lose it, and whoever loses their life for my sake will find it. (Matt. 10:37–39)

For whoever does the will of my Father in heaven is my brother and sister and mother. (Matt. 12:50)

I submit to Jesus as my Lord because I love Him, because I want to reverence Him, and because He is the most important One in my life. I realize the massive debt for which He has forgiven me and I understand the treasure that He has given to me: the ability to have a relationship with God, to know Him personally here now, to have access to the Holy of holies, to be able to pray, to be able to have faith, to be part of His kingdom on earth, and to have life with Him in heaven forever! I understand that Jesus loved me so much that He took the punishment I deserved and that I deserved hell, not heaven. Because I love Him and out of deep gratitude for all Jesus has done for me, I can't help but say, "Yes, Lord," to anything He asks me to do! He gives me the desire, freedom, strength, and power to obey His Word in every area of my life.

I long to obey Him, even when I don't understand what He is asking me to do, even if I don't agree with it, even if the world gets offended. I must obey Him even if no one else does. I cannot look into the eyes of my Lord Jesus, blazing with such great love, mercy, and grace for me—knowing what He did for me on the cross—and say defiantly, "No, Lord!" Now, I can only joyfully say, "Yes, Lord," even if it costs me dearly—even if it costs me *everything*. He gave everything for me, now I have the joy and privilege of giving everything for Him. I want more than anything to hear Him say to me one day, "Well done, good and faithful servant" (Matt. 25:23). No one else's approval matters anymore. I "put on the new self, created to be like God in true righteousness and holiness" (Eph. 4:24).

Because I have died to my old self according to God's Word in Romans 6, I have died to my will, my goals, my greatest dreams, my plans, my priorities, and my wisdom. That is all nailed to the cross. I was crucified with Christ and buried with Him. This is historical fact in God's sight. God placed me in Christ so that what happened to Him also happened to me. The old sinful me died to this world and was buried. God raised me to a new life in Christ when Jesus rose from the dead. He gave me a new spirit. Everything I have belongs to Jesus and everything He has belongs to me. Wow! Let that sink in. Now, I am a living sacrifice for Jesus. I am alive to His Spirit, His will, His goals, His dreams, His plans, His priorities, and His wisdom. My goals now are to love the Lord my God with all my heart, mind, soul, and strength (Luke 10:27); to bring Him great glory by walking in obedience to Him through His Spirit's power; and to love others with His love.

> "I am a living sacrifice for Jesus.
> I am alive to His Spirit, His will,
> His goals, His dreams, His plans,
> His priorities, and His wisdom."

WAYS I DISRESPECTED GOD

If those in human authority in this life deserve respect, how much more the omnipotent Creator of the entire universe deserves my greatest reverence and honor. He is the King of kings and Lord of lords! We have focused much on how approachable God is and the access we have to Him through Christ. But we cannot ever lose sight of the fact that our God is a great God. He is worthy of the utmost respect. I unknowingly used to do a lot of disrespectful things to God.

- I questioned God's wisdom.
- I questioned His authority.
- I tried to reshape God to be who I wanted Him to be (or thought He was) instead of accepting Him as He presents Himself in the Bible.
- I disrespected God's authority over me and tried to go around it.
- I had selfish motives.
- I implied that God was not enough for me by trying to find contentment in other things.
- I tried to tell God what to do.
- I wanted emotional connection with God but I didn't honor and respect God's holiness and majesty properly.
- I had a small picture of God and a huge picture of myself; my spiritual vision was warped and distorted.
- I thought I could accomplish the Holy Spirit's job in my own life and for other people.
- I disobeyed many of God's commands and didn't even realize it.
- I cherished sin in my heart.
- I didn't truly trust God. I trusted myself. I lived in fear, anxiety, and worry—as if everything was up to me.
- I did not understand God's sovereignty. That was the biggest key that opened up peace for me—studying God's sovereignty and realizing I was not God! His responsibilities do not belong to me.

WAYS I CAN RESPECT AND REVERENCE GOD

Thankfully, God is pretty explicit about how He desires us to show our love and honor for Him. His Word reveals His heart to us, and He tells us how to please Him and exactly in what manner we are to approach Him. Here are a few examples of ways I can show proper fear and reverence toward God when Christ is my Savior and Lord:

- Honor His authority and the authority of His Word (Matt. 28:18; John 1:1).
- Obey Him in everything (John 14:23–24).
- Speak respectfully of Him and to Him (Heb. 12:28).
- Don't take His name in vain (Exod. 20:7).
- Honor the authority structure He has set up in my life in the government, the church, the workplace, and the family (Luke 20:25; Rom. 13:1–7; 1 Cor. 11:3; Eph. 5:22–33).
- Accept God as He presents Himself and don't try to change Him to be what I want Him to be (Isa. 48:17).
- Praise God for all of His amazing qualities and His character (Ps. 149:1).
- Rejoice in Him always, pray continually, and thank God in all circumstances, for this is God's will for me (1 Thess. 5:16–18).
- Focus on the good (Phil. 4:8).
- Don't complain or argue (Phil. 2:14–16).
- Trust Him no matter what happens. Even as I suffer I can worship Him, thank Him, trust Him, and not sin against Him by accusing Him of wrongdoing (Hab. 3:17–19; Job 1:20-22).
- Abide in Christ and in His Word (John 15:1–8).
- Sing praises and hymns of thanksgiving to Him continually in my heart (Pss. 95:1–11; 150:1–6; 1 Thess. 5:16–18).
- Share the truth, love, mercy, and grace of God with others, making disciples with His truth by His power for His glory alone (Matt. 28:18–20).

God desires all believers (men and women) to submit ourselves fully to Christ as *Lord* of our lives. We often use that word *Lord* so casually. This should not be! Lordship is a totally life-changing thing. My Lord is in charge of my decisions and the direction of everything in my life! He is the Boss. Submitting ourselves to the lordship of Christ is where real Christian submission always starts. We follow the example of Jesus Christ, Himself. Though He was God, Jesus submitted Himself to God the Father. He said, "Not my will, but yours be done" (Luke 22:42). That is the essence of a submissive spirit. Jesus was and is God, but in love He submitted His will completely to His Father's will. All three persons of the Godhead are of equal value and worth. Submission is not about value. Jesus does not have less worth because He submits to God the Father.

> "Submission is about the authority structure God puts in place in relationships for our good, provision, protection, and blessing and to provide order."

This is where we often get confused and angry. We think that whoever submits is somehow worth less than the person in the position of authority. That is not how God views submission at all. Submission is about the authority structure God puts in place in relationships for our good, provision, protection, and blessing and to provide order (Rom. 13:1–7). This includes the authority that governments have over their citizens, the authority that a boss has over her employee, the authority that church leaders have over their congregation, the authority that parents have over their underage children, and the authority that husbands have in marriage. God holds those in delegated positions of authority accountable and responsible to Himself for how they care for, lead, protect, and nurture those who are placed under their care. Only

God has absolute authority. No human has absolute authority over another person. God does not ever condone sin against others or abuse of others by anyone in a position of authority. Leaders will be held to a higher standard when they face God at Judgment Day.

If Christ is Lord, then I must carefully examine my heart, with God's help, for anything I am putting above Him. We are all prone to idolatry, but today our idols are often so subtle we don't even realize what we are doing. I love what my single sister in Christ shared about how God asked her to give up her idol:

I remember when God asked me to give up my dreams. "Okay God, Your will and not mine. Done! I will go wherever you want and do whatever you want," I prayed. I was excited about the direction God had planned for my life. It took me a few variations of this conversation to understand what He meant. He meant my most personal and valuable dream. He wanted me to take my desire to become a wife and a mother and lay it on the altar. I begged God to take any dream but that one. I pleaded with Him, offering Him anything in exchange for the chance to hold on to my dream. My terms have never been sufficient. My dying to self had to be on His terms alone. I remember the day, broken beyond anything I can put into words, when I finally laid my dream on the altar. At first I laid it on the altar, but I could not walk away. I laid it down, but kept my fingers on it. This was not good enough. God asked me to walk away from the dream, the idol. I turned my back on my dream and felt paralyzed. How do you move forward and away from the only thing you cherished for so long? I allowed myself to live with the hope of a fairy tale coming true.

I was confused and did not understand how God could want me to stop hoping. Wasn't He a God of hope? He most certainly is! He had to teach me, ever so slowly, that my hope is to be in Him alone, not the promise of a man. He did not want me to stop hoping; He wanted me to stop hoping in anything other than Him to fill my deepest desire.

He wanted to become my deepest desire. Then, and only then, could He fill that void.

• First, I had to realize He was not my greatest desire.
• Then, I had to realize that He was my greatest desire.

Giving up the dream of marriage and babies was one of the most painful things I have ever done in my life.

Just like my dear single friend had to give up her dream in order to embrace God's will, God calls each follower of Christ to give up his or her dreams and to lay them on the altar before Him. We don't know ahead of time if we will receive those dreams back or not. I had to lay down my dreams of a perfect marriage, my husband's attention, my feeling loved, my being in control, and my fears about scary things that could happen. Would I trust God with all of my fears and dreams without any reservation or hesitation? Would I allow Him to be Lord of every part of my life? Was He the most important desire in my heart?

Dreams are not bad things, but when we mis-prioritize them, they can easily turn into idols. I know using the word *idols* sounds so strange and like it would not apply to any of us today because we don't bow down to statues, but idols are any things or people that we cherish more than Christ. They are those things that we think we must have in order to be content in life. They are sometimes our greatest dreams and they are the things upon which we base our worth and identity. We can make anything into an idol: control, self, happiness, beauty, power, money, marriage, spouse, children, popularity, health, politics, etc. Idols are the things we trust most to protect us and to meet our deepest needs instead of placing all of our trust and hope in God. They can be the things we most fear losing. Sometimes our idols are very good things—they are just in the wrong place in our lives.

MARRIAGE AS A REFLECTION OF CHRIST'S LORDSHIP

So many things about how I can respect and reverence God translate into ways I can also show respect and honor for my husband. Husbands are not deity, of course, but there are parallels between one's relationship to Christ and one's marriage. God uses marriage to demonstrate the intimacy and type of relationship He desires to have with us through Christ.

> *Lord,*
>
> *As I am about to read some Scripture passages, please open my spiritual eyes and ears that I might see and hear all that You are saying to me as a woman. Replace my thoughts with Your thoughts. Replace my desires with Your desires. Help me to confront faulty ideas I have about godly marriage, godly masculinity, and godly femininity. Help me to reject the world's lies and choose to believe, embrace, and practice the truth that is found in the Bible. Give me great courage and boldness to become the woman You created me to be. Allow me to greatly bless You, my husband, and my children as I submit myself completely to Your will and Your truth. I pray that You might transform me to be more and more like Christ, by the power of Your Spirit. Accomplish Your will and Your greatest glory through me! I long to be close to You and to know You more than anything.*
>
> *In the name and power of Christ, amen!*

Carefully read and meditate on the following passages, focusing on the commands God gives to us as wives.

Wives, submit to your own husbands as you do to the Lord. For the husband is the head of the wife as Christ is the head of the church, his body, of which he is the Savior. Now as the church submits to Christ, so also wives should submit to their husbands in everything. Husbands, love your wives, just as Christ loved the church and gave himself up for her to make her holy, cleansing her by the washing with water through the word, and to present her to himself as a radiant church, without stain or wrinkle or any other blemish, but holy and blameless. In this same way, husbands ought to love their wives as their own bodies. He who loves his wife loves himself. After all, no one ever hated their own body, but they feed and care for their body, just as Christ does the church—for we are members of his body. "For this reason a man will leave his father and mother and be united to his wife, and the two will become one flesh." This is a profound mystery—but I am talking about Christ and the church. However, each one of you also must love his wife as he loves himself, and the wife must respect her husband. (Eph. 5:22–33)

> "Each one of you also must love his wife as he loves himself, and the wife must respect her husband." (Eph. 5:33)

But I want you to realize that the head of every man is Christ, and the head of the woman is man, and the head of Christ is God. (1 Cor. 11:3)

Teach the older women to be reverent in the way they live, not to be slanderers or addicted to much wine, but to teach what is good. Then they can urge the younger women to love their

husbands and children, to be self-controlled and pure, to be
busy at home, to be kind, and to be subject to their husbands,
so that no one will malign the word of God. (Titus 2:3–5)

Wives, in the same way submit yourselves to your own husbands so that, if any of them do not believe the word, they may
be won over without words by the behavior of their wives, when
they see the purity and reverence of your lives. Your beauty
should not come from outward adornment, such as elaborate hairstyles and the wearing of gold jewelry or fine clothes.
Rather, it should be that of your inner self, the unfading beauty
of a gentle and quiet spirit, which is of great worth in God's
sight. For this is the way the holy women of the past who put
their hope in God used to adorn themselves. They submitted
themselves to their own husbands, like Sarah, who obeyed
Abraham and called him her lord. You are her daughters if
you do what is right and do not give way to fear. Husbands, in
the same way be considerate as you live with your wives, and
treat them with respect as the weaker partner and as heirs with
you of the gracious gift of life, so that nothing will hinder your
prayers. (1 Peter 3:1–7)

Because I am only writing for wives, I am not going to elaborate
much on a godly husband's role in marriage. As we move into the next
chapters, my focus will be the commands God has given to wives to
submit to our husbands and to respect them, and our own obedience
to, respect for, and submission to Christ. Much more is at stake in our
marriages than we may realize. I want to be sure that we all catch this:
according to Titus 2:5, when a Christian wife does not cooperate with
her husband's leadership, the Word of God is maligned (unless the
husband is asking the wife to sin or he is not in his right mind or is
abusing her or her children). Yikes! This is much bigger than just one

person, one marriage, or one family. This is about the reputation of God's Word and Christ Himself. My refusal to follow my husband's God-given leadership hurts the gospel, hurts the name of Christ, and repels unbelievers from finding the real love and real life that is only available in Jesus.

God's Beautiful Design

Husbands and wives both ought to receive and give love and respect in marriage. God does command husbands to honor their wives (1 Peter 3:7) in addition to loving them. God also commands wives to love their husbands (Titus 2:3–5) in addition to respecting and submitting to them. God also commands all believers to love all people with His unconditional love (Matt. 22:39; 1 Cor. 13:4–8). Part of Christian love is treating others with respect. But God, in His infinite wisdom, gives a special emphasis to wives to respect and submit to their husbands and a special emphasis to husbands to selflessly love their wives as Christ loves the church. Maybe both husbands and wives have areas where God would like for us to grow to become the men and women He desires us to be.

What Biblical Submission Means

In Scripture, the word "submit" is a military term that means, "to place oneself under in rank." God commands all believers to submit to the government, to their church leaders, and to their employers, unless that person in authority asks us to sin (Rom. 13:1–7; Eph. 6:5–9; Heb. 13:17). If I were in the military, I would voluntarily place myself under the authority of my superior officer in the chain of command. This is a picture of the way a private in the army honors the leadership of his corporal. The corporal answers to her sergeant and the chain of command continues up to the five-star general. Even the five-star general answers to a higher authority, the president, who is the commander in chief. Everyone must know his or her place in the chain of command and honor the authority given to those in positions of authority.

The only time a corporal would not submit to the sergeant above her would be if the sergeant was asking her to do something immoral, unethical, illegal, or in direct defiance to the commands and protocol that have been given by those higher in the chain of authority. A soldier's submission is based on his or her respect for the uniform, authority, and position given to those above him or her. Submission in the military is not based on someone's personal feelings, nor is it about agreement. Without a proper chain of command, there is chaos. Soldiers' and civilians' lives may be endangered if the authority in the chain of command is ignored. This chain of command and proper understanding of submission to authority is what allows the army to accomplish its primary mission of destroying the enemy and protecting the nation in times of war.

In *Recovering Biblical Manhood and Womanhood*, Wayne Grudem and John Piper define biblical submission:

> Submission refers to a wife's divine calling to honor and affirm her husband's leadership and help carry it through according to her gifts. It is not an absolute surrender of her will. Rather, we speak of her disposition to yield to her husband's guidance and her inclination to follow his leadership. Christ is her absolute authority, not her husband.[1]

Grudem and Piper also define biblical headship:

> In the home, biblical headship is the husband's divine calling to take primary responsibility for Christlike leadership,

protection, and provision. . . . We stress . . . sacrificial headship that keeps the good of the wife in view and regards her as a joint heir of the grace of life (1 Peter 3:7); and we stress thoughtful submission that does not make the husband an absolute lord.[2]

There is a chain of command in God's design for the family that is given to us by God in His Word (1 Cor. 11:3; Eph. 6:1–2; Col. 3:18–19) that looks like this:

God the Father > Jesus Christ > husband > wife > underage children

Children answer to their parents—but ultimately, both children and parents answer to God. Even Jesus the Son answers to God the Father. No human being is ever the final authority. God is the final authority. His Word has final authority. God calls husbands to live in total submission to Christ just as He calls every believer (male and female) to live in total submission to Christ as Lord (James 4:7). Thankfully, for wives already married to unbelievers, God is able to use an unbelieving husband to lead a believing wife, just as He is able to direct the course of a pagan king's decisions to lead His people: "In the Lord's hand the king's heart is a stream of water that he channels toward all who please him" (Prov. 21:1). (For those who are still single, please choose only to marry a believer according to 1 Corinthians 7:39 and 2 Corinthians 6:14.)

We are living in times of spiritual warfare. This chain of command that God gave to us existed before the fall, but how much more critical it is now as we face a great spiritual enemy that we honor God's chain of command for our ultimate good, protection, and provision; for the good of our families; for the good of the church; and for spreading the gospel.

Respect and submission are freely given.

A wife's biblical submission to her husband and her respect for him are things that she does *voluntarily* out of obedience and submission to God, because she wants to honor Christ as Lord. Her obedience to God is not something that can be forced, demanded, or coerced any more than a wife can force her husband to love her as God commands him to. God does not command husbands to make their wives submit to them. He does not command wives to force their husbands to love them. A wife may certainly ask her husband to love her, but she cannot control him. A husband may certainly ask his wife to honor his leadership and cooperate with him according to Scripture, but neither spouse has the "right" in Christ to abuse the other in any way, or to force anyone into anything. Ultimately, we are each responsible for our own obedience to God. It is not any person's right to attempt to override a grown adult's free will—that is control, tyranny, oppression, or manipulation. It is not the love or design of God. Each believer will receive rewards in heaven for living in obedience to God. Those who do not follow Christ and who do not do His will are going to receive God's just and righteous condemnation for their rebellion against God according to Scripture.

> A good man brings good things out of the good stored up in him, and an evil man brings evil things out of the evil stored up in him. But I tell you that everyone will have to give account on the day of judgment for every empty word they have spoken. For by your words you will be acquitted, and by your words you will be condemned. (Matt. 12:35–37)

> By the grace God has given me, I laid a foundation as a wise builder, and someone else is building on it. But each one should build with care. For no one can lay any foundation other than the one already laid, which is Jesus Christ. If anyone builds on this foundation using gold, silver, costly stones, wood, hay or straw, their work will be shown for what it is, because the Day will bring it to light. It will be revealed with fire, and the fire

will test the quality of each person's work. If what has been built survives, the builder will receive a reward. If it is burned up, the builder will suffer loss but yet will be saved—even though only as one escaping through the flames. (1 Cor. 3:10–15)

He will punish those who do not know God and do not obey the gospel of our Lord Jesus. They will be punished with everlasting destruction and shut out from the presence of the Lord and from the glory of his might on the day he comes to be glorified in his holy people and to be marveled at among all those who have believed. (2 Thess. 1:8–10)

Each partner has equal value and equal importance.

An illustration that fits marriage very well, in my mind, is the picture of a team competing in pairs figure skating in the Olympics. One partner cannot compete without the other—each has equal value and importance—but each also has a specific role. The man does the lifting and the woman has the more glamorous role of being lifted high into the air as she spins and twirls. Can you imagine what would happen if they tried to reverse these roles? (I picture lots of injuries and no medals.) Both partners listen to the authority of their coach. The woman follows the lead of her male partner as they skate to create something so much more beautiful than either could accomplish on his or her own. The woman is not "oppressed" because she fulfills her feminine role in the figure skating pair. She is honored and exalted. She soars to new heights on her partner's shoulders. Their coach is honored by their beautiful performance, their entire country is blessed by their teamwork, and they bring home a medal for their nation.

This is very similar to a Christian marriage. Each of our marriages is on display before the world and all of history. When we each fulfill the role God has given us as either husband or wife, we bring great glory and honor to Him, to His gospel, to our brothers and sisters in Christ, to ourself, to our spouse, and to our children.

WHAT BIBLICAL SUBMISSION IS NOT

Some wives worry that they might be demeaned if they honor their husband as the head of the home. They are afraid they will lose their power and their "voice" in the relationship. They may also be alarmed and think that God's design for loving male headship is the same thing as male domination. These are important concerns to address. From my own experience, I am still very ambitious and driven—a go-getter with strong opinions, ideas, personal convictions, and feelings. I still retain my intelligence, gifts, talents, abilities, personality, and strengths. But I no longer try to control my husband or demand my own way. I strive to show my husband genuine respect. I joyfully, willingly place myself under Greg's God-given authority, protection, provision, and leadership in our marriage. I put all of my strength, drive, ambition, power, and motivation at God's disposal to support Greg—to bless him, to lift him up, to build him up, to inspire him, and to work with him as a teammate to make him and our marriage a success by God's definition. I apply myself to God's priorities and operate in the parameters of Greg's leadership knowing that God will lead me through my husband. I seek God's will over my own now. Life is not about getting what I want. It is primarily about God's glory. Paradoxically, that is the place where I will find the greatest possible joy, fulfillment, blessing, and peace.

"Life is not about getting what I want.
It is primarily about God's glory.
Paradoxically, that is the place where
I will find the greatest possible joy,
fulfillment, blessing, and peace."

It is important to clarify what biblical submission is *not*, because the world uses the word "submission" in a very derogatory way that means, essentially, "slavery," and I don't want anyone to think that the Bible commands wives to be slaves. Sometimes I wish we could use an entirely different word, just to prevent this confusion.

Submission is not completely mutual.

A husband may certainly decide to submit to his wife's preference or her concerns for her benefit but a husband does not submit to his wife in the same sense that a wife submits to her husband. There is a very popular view that is held by many Christians today that Ephesians 5:21 ("Submit to one another out of reverence for Christ") is God's real design for marriage and that submission is to be identical between husbands and wives. "Mutual submission" says that husbands and wives have equal authority from God in marriage and that each is required to submit to the other if there is a disagreement.

If we read the entire chapter of Ephesians 5, we see that Paul is giving instructions to the church about how to treat one another in the church. The section on marriage begins in verse 22. Some editors of English versions have included verse 21 with the verses afterward, which makes it look like that verse goes with the verses about marriage. But when the Bible was written there were no verse numbers or headings. It is always important to take a verse in proper context.[3] It is also vital that we remember that God gave leaders to the church (pastors, deacons, elders, and teachers) and that God directs the congregation to submit to their authority in ways that God does not expect leaders to submit to the congregation (1 Thess. 5:12; Heb. 13:17). There are some issues where believers can all submit to one another in the sense that they seek the good of others or the preferences of others above themselves—but we do not compromise biblical principles. For example, one person might prefer traditional hymns, but she might encourage others to enjoy contemporary praise music and not complain about it because she knows that other people prefer that style. Our submission to one another in the body of Christ does not negate the authority of the leaders of the church and this command does not give everyone in the congregation the same spiritual authority as the pastor or another leader would have.

In marriage, while it is true that a husband might "submit to his wife" in a sense of being humble and selfless, his submission is not the same as hers. He does not submit to his wife in the sense that she is in a position of authority over him. He submits to Christ and dies to self as he seeks God's best and His will for his wife and family. If the couple has a disagreement, he ultimately bears the weight of responsibility and accountability to God for the decision that is made, just as God held Adam accountable as the leader in the garden of Eden when he and Eve sinned. In order for us to conclude that mutual submission is God's design, we would have to choose to apply that particular verse that does not mention marriage at the expense of all of the other verses that are explicitly about marriage later in the chapter and in a number of other passages.

Submission is not agreement.

Some husbands insist that for a wife to "properly submit," she must always agree with her husband. I see nowhere in Scripture that God requires us to agree with Him when we submit to His lordship. He asks us to trust Him and to have faith in Him even when we don't understand, but that is not the same thing as demanding that we agree with Him. I see nowhere in Scripture where anyone who submits to a human God-given authority (even a child or a person in the deplorable circumstances of slavery) is required to agree with the person in authority. In fact, we, as believers, are called upon to submit intelligently to those in authority over us and we are to refuse to submit to anyone who asks us to sin against God.

Submission is not about the husband being "right."

My submission to my husband's authority—or any person's God-given authority over me—is not about that person being right. No human is infallible. Only God is perfect. All humans sin and make mistakes. For me to submit to my husband as a believing wife means that I trust God more than I trust my husband or myself. It is about my submission to the lordship of Christ and my trust in God's sovereignty to lead me through my imperfect husband. That is how I can have perfect peace as my husband leads me even if I don't agree with a particular decision. My understanding of Ephesians 5:22–33 is that a wife submits to her husband as she does to Christ. If someone in a position of God-given authority tries to lead a believer to severely violate God's Word, "We must obey God rather than human beings!" (Acts 5:29). However, if we choose to obey God rather than people, we must be prepared for the consequences of our actions here on earth.

> "If my husband asks me to blatantly defy God's Word and to sin, then I must obey God rather than my husband."

Some examples of this are Daniel, his friends, and the apostles. Daniel refused to bow to the king's idol and faced the lions' den. Daniel's three friends refused to worship the king and were thrown into the fiery furnace. The apostles all refused to stop preaching in the name of Christ, and eleven of them were martyred. All of them were severely persecuted by the Jewish religious authorities. In most cultures today, if a wife resists her husband's God-given authority, that does not mean she will experience capital punishment, but a wife is accountable to God if she decides to go against her husband. I would certainly not want to resist my husband over something minor. I would personally have to believe my husband was asking me to commit a very clear sin for me to be willing to refuse to submit to him. Such a situation has never happened in the seven years since I have been practicing biblical submission. I thank and praise God for that blessing. However, if my husband asks me to blatantly defy God's Word and to sin, then I must obey God rather than my husband. Only God's authority is absolute. For example, if my husband says to kill, steal, commit idolatry, have an abortion, join a cult, molest children, cover up a crime for him, watch pornography, have a threesome, put him before God, and so on, I would have to refuse Greg and obey God instead. Hopefully, situations like this would be pretty rare for believing wives. If it is just that I don't agree with Greg or we have a difference of interpretation in Scripture, I may share my heart, perspective, and feelings, but then I must trust God to lead Greg to make the best decision. Just because I don't agree with my husband does not necessarily mean he is wrong. My disagreement is not an excuse for me to disobey God's Word.

Submission does not mean I can't have my own opinion.

If I always agreed with Greg, that wouldn't be "submission," it would be agreement. Biblical submission happens when I acknowledge the authority of Christ to determine what is best for me even when I don't understand how He is going to work all things out for my good, and even if I don't agree with a particular decision at the time. I am my husband's most important advisor, his closest friend, his confidante, his partner, his teammate, and his ally. He will likely cherish my ideas, feelings, insights, needs, and suggestions if I respect him and cooperate with his leadership. We, being human, are not in a position to always see clearly what decision is right, or even best, at a given time. Our wisdom and vision are flawed. Only God can see the whole picture.

> Trust in the LORD with all your heart and lean not on your own understanding. (Prov. 3:5)

> Nothing in all creation is hidden from God's sight. Everything is uncovered and laid bare before the eyes of him to whom we must give account. (Heb. 4:13)

In God's design, a person exercising God-given authority (in the government, at church, in the workplace, or in the home) is about:

- Accepting responsibility for those precious people entrusted to the one in authority (Heb. 13:17)
- Being accountable to God (Heb. 13:17)
- Seeking God's wisdom (2 Chron. 1:10)
- Protecting and defending God's people (Rom. 13:1–5)
- Providing for God's people (John 21:15–17)
- Loving people with God's unconditional love (1 Cor. 13:4–8)
- Establishing order instead of chaos (Rom. 13:1–5)
- Leading through serving (Luke 22:24–27)

Submission is not an invitation to abuse.

When a wife shows genuine respect, honor, and submission to a man who is in his right mind, he will eventually tend to respond by desiring to honor, serve, and love her more. That is how God wired men to respond when someone, especially a woman, shows them honor and true respect. There is no guarantee, of course, that every husband will eventually change, just like there is no guarantee that if a husband loves his wife as Christ loves the church and seeks to lead her in a godly way that his wife will respect and honor him and his leadership. Sometimes one spouse must persist in obedience to God without seeing any earthly results for many years, perhaps even for a lifetime. Thankfully, obedience to God is its own reward both now and in eternity. However, Greg was never tempted to mistreat me when I treated him well. That wouldn't make sense. It is similar to the way God has wired women; a woman who feels loved by her husband wants to show honor and respect. A wife whose husband loves her with the love of God will want to treat him as well as she possibly can out of gratitude for all he has done for her. God's design generally produces a win/win for everyone in time. Still, no matter what happens, a wife's motives are to be simply to love and please God as she seeks to bless her husband.

Unfortunately, there are sometimes leaders in positions of authority who abuse or mistreat those they are sworn to protect, serve, lead, provide for, and care for. That is *wrong!* I cannot emphasize this enough. God will repay those who misuse the authority He gave to them. They will stand before Him and give an account and He will dispense justice (eternal condemnation in hell) unless they repent, turn to Christ, and receive mercy through the blood of Jesus in this lifetime. Either an abusive husband will pay dearly for his sin, or Jesus will pay dearly for his sin. All will eventually be made right. If a leader is abusing his authority, there are supposed to be other leaders in place in the church, work environment, and government who will help those who are dealing with true abuse and correct and/or punish the guilty. As a dear minister we know shared about spiritual authority, "A godly man will always respond to being in a position of authority with great humility. He will desire to seek God's wisdom so that he makes the best possible decisions for everyone in his care." It is never God's design for a husband to lord his position over his wife or for a husband to be a selfish, cruel, hateful, vengeful tyrant who demands to be served. That is a severe distortion of the model Jesus gave to those to whom He entrusts authority.

Jesus said to them, "The kings of the Gentiles lord it over them . . . But you are not to be like that. Instead, the greatest among you should be like the youngest, and the one who rules like the one who serves. For who is greater, the one who is at the table or the one who serves? Is it not the one who is at the table? But I am among you as one who serves." (Luke 22:25–27)

Submission is not oppression.

I approached my marriage from the world's perspective and my own wisdom for almost fifteen years. I tried to carry all the weight and responsibility for the marriage and family and was stressed, worried, afraid, and upset many times. I felt like the only adult in the family. I thought I had to do everything while my husband avoided responsibility and became increasingly emotionally distant, passive, and unplugged. I worked full-time until we had children, then I worked twenty hours per week and also did almost all of the housework, all of the cooking, all of the finances, all of the discipline for the children, and all of the child care every moment that I was home. My husband sat in front of a screen silently, or worked on the house. I was overloaded, overworked, stressed out, and seething with resentment and bitterness. Greg was deeply hurting, too, but I didn't have any idea that I had hurt him.

The world says that God's ways are oppressive. The truth is that trying to carry a burden you were not designed to carry is oppressive. The truth is that being consumed by worry, anxiety, and fear every waking moment is oppressive. The truth is that living under the control of sin instead of by the power of the Spirit of God is real slavery and oppression. When God's Spirit controls my life, I have all of the fruit of the Spirit in increasing measure every day: love, joy, peace, patience, kindness, goodness, gentleness, faithfulness, and self-control (Gal. 5:22–23). That is freedom! That is blessing. That is real power. I have never felt more loved, cherished, nurtured, and blessed to be Greg's wife than I have these last few years of our marriage. Things feel right. The marriage runs smoothly. There is no more contention, division, or tension. The walls are gone. God has restored intimacy on every level. We are both so thankful for God's wisdom and His ways. We are both much more the people we have always wanted to be. The only thing we are "deprived of" now is the power of sin that used to destroy us.

> "The world says that God's ways are oppressive. . . . The truth is that living under the control of sin instead of by the power of the Spirit of God is real slavery and oppression."

For either a husband or a wife to lord power over the other spouse would be sinful and contrary to God's good design for marriage. Male domination—where a husband forcefully asserts dominance in physically, emotionally, or spiritually abusive ways and treats his wife harshly without godly love—is a sinful distortion of male headship. A wife becoming slave-like is also a sinful distortion that undermines the value, dignity, beauty, and worth of a wife and warps the picture of what godly femininity is supposed to be. Male passivity is a sinful distortion of biblical masculinity that abandons God-given responsibility and accountability and endangers a man's wife and family.

In *Recovering Biblical Manhood and Womanhood*, John Piper and Wayne Grudem assert that "male domination is a personal moral failure, not a biblical doctrine."[4] Grudem and Piper go on to say that feminism declares that there is no distinction between male dominance and male headship and that the only way for a woman to not be oppressed by a man is that she must have an equal position, identical role, and identical power in marriage. Unfortunately, headship is a singular position. Two people cannot both be in charge. Certainly part of godly leadership is that a husband would wisely delegate many things to his intelligent wife's care and responsibility, but he is to retain the ultimate responsibility and accountability before God to lead the family. If a wife attempts to take over her husband's position, either the husband will fight his wife for his rightful place in God's order or the husband will give up his position and let his wife take over as he does nothing, respecting her as being in authority over the family and relinquishing his responsibility.

When a woman dominates and rules over her husband, making demands and expecting him to respond in obedience, that is also a warped, sinful distortion of both masculinity and femininity. At best, children grow up to often repeat the patterns of masculinity, femininity, and marriage they witnessed because what they saw becomes normal to them. Sons will likely become passive husbands and daughters will likely be dominating in their future marriages. Any time a marriage is a sinful distortion of God's design, this creates tension, strife, and pain in the marriage, and for children in their current family and in their future family relationships. Sadly, when a child witnesses role reversals, or a mother's domination with a father's passive response, these dynamics can sometimes help to promote a lifetime of gender confusion in children (as we are currently seeing in our largely feminist culture today).[5]

When people insist that men and women are the same in every way and that marriage roles are interchangeable and identical, one danger is that male and female sexuality and expression in every aspect of life become "interchangeable," which fosters homosexuality, bisexuality, and acceptance of transgender ideology. I know that may sound extreme to those who haven't studied the history of the feminist movement, but here are a few of the purposeful goals of "the first, second, and third waves of feminism" in our culture: Feminism promotes the destruction of the traditional concept of marriage and family, the destruction of God's gender roles in marriage, the separation of biology from the concept of family, divorce, abortion, the idea that children are a burden to women, an androgynous society where everyone is the same, "gender fluidity" (people can choose for themselves if they want to be male or female and change back and forth at any time), sex outside of God's design (including "hooking up," cohabitation, homosexuality, and bisexuality), undermining the authority of God's Word, and undermining the existence and character of God Himself.[6]

We have been marinating in these ideas all of our lives. The idea that "men and women are exactly the same" isn't true based on God's Word, neuroscience, anthropology, world history, or personal experience. The results of a society embracing the concept that men and women are exactly the same are oppressive; God's plans are not. Men and women can each go to sinful extremes that are outside of God's design, creating great pain in marriages and families and unfathomable consequences for generations to come. How precious God's design is for masculinity, femininity, and marriage—not just for ourselves but also for future generations and the stability of the family, the church, and our nations. Our families are the building blocks of society. Strong families and marriages benefit us all and bring glory to God as we approach things with God's higher wisdom.

Submission is not absolute.

God instructs us to submit to our husbands "as you do to the Lord" or "as is fitting in the Lord" (Eph. 5:22; Col. 3:18). It is my belief—based on my understanding of what Scripture teaches about human authority—that a wife is not required by God to submit to a husband who is not in his right mind (whether drunk, high, or clearly mentally ill), involved in unrepentant adultery, involved in immoral illegal activity, or abusing her or her children, or where there are certain other severe issues. A wife can fervently pray for God to bring her husband to conviction and repentance if her husband is involved in unrepentant sin. She may need to get somewhere safe if she is not safe. She will need to be very sensitive to God's Spirit and seek godly, trusted, experienced counsel to help her navigate these kinds of severe issues. She may need to involve the police, legal counsel, or medical help, depending on the situation. She can pray for her husband to be restored to Christ and for eventual healing and reconciliation of the marriage and family. She can carry herself in a godly way and treat her husband with respect and honor. But she may need to wait until her husband has shown true repentance, transparency, a healthy mind, and a willingness to work to restore lost trust before she can begin to submit to him and live with him again. God never commands us to trust someone who is untrustworthy. We can always trust God, but there are times when we cannot trust a man. A husband may need godly counseling and mentoring by a wise, mature man in the church. The couple may need counseling together. There are times when a husband has not changed and a wife may have to stay on her own (1 Cor. 7:10–16), but her goal will be to see healing for her husband spiritually, for their marriage covenant, for herself, and for their children.

No husband, wife, or child should ever feel unsafe in his or her family's home. Those who twist Scripture to say that wives or husbands should dominate their spouses, mistreat others, or abuse others, and who demand that men or women be treated as children or "second-class citizens" grossly distort the Word of God to their great shame. God never condones any sin or mistreatment against anyone.*

A wife does have the ability to express herself and to set limits on herself if her husband asks her to do something she truly can't do. If my husband says, "Help me carry this three-hundred-pound couch outside and lift it up into the truck," I would have to say, "I would really love to be able to help you, but I am just not that strong." I don't think my husband would ask me to do something like this, but if a man asks his wife to do something that is seriously not possible for her or beyond her abilities or that would actually endanger herself or others, I would hope that she would speak up about that. In such situations, a wife may need to say, "I wish I could help with this, but I really can't. Is there another way we can reach this goal that I am capable of doing?"

If a husband asks his wife to go against God's Word, she will need to respectfully refuse to cooperate. A husband is not above God. God is the ultimate authority and we will answer to Him, as will our men.

Submission is not related to value.

Submission in the Bible has nothing to do with a person's value: "There is neither Jew nor Gentile, neither slave nor free, nor is there male and female, for you are all one in Christ Jesus" (Gal. 3:28). All

---

*Greg and I also believe that BDSM (practices involving bondage, discipline, sadism, or masochism) as well as so-called "Christian domestic discipline" fall into the realm of distortions of God's design for marriage. We do not condone or support these lifestyles or practices. Thankfully, our God is mighty to save and to heal!

people are of equal value in God's sight. We are also all equally created as image bearers of God as human beings—both male and female (Gen. 1:27). The world assigns a greater dollar value to those who lead in the government, the military, and corporations. But from God's perspective, the value of all human life is equal. An unborn baby's life is just as precious to God as the value of the life of the president of the United States of America. A child's life is just as precious as a parent's life. A citizen's life is just as valuable as a five-star general's life. A wife's life and value to God is equal to a husband's life and value in His sight. It is time to get rid of the worldly idea that authority is what determines a person's value and that if we submit to authority, then we have less or no value.

> "All people are of equal value in God's sight. We are also all equally created as image bearers of God as human beings—both male and female."

WHAT BIBLICAL SUBMISSION ACCOMPLISHES

I once had a job as a pharmacy manager at a grocery store chain. My staff pharmacist, Teresa, was "under my authority." She checked with me before making major decisions because I was ultimately accountable for the decisions in that pharmacy. I always listened to her great ideas and then tried to make the best decision I could. Teresa was a dear friend and a wise advisor. Really, she was much smarter than I was! I cherished her insights. Many times I did what she suggested; sometimes I didn't. She wasn't upset about that. She respected my authority as the manager. A few years later both of us were working for a different retail pharmacy chain, but this time our roles were reversed. She was the manager, so I always checked with her and did things the way she thought was best because she had authority in that situation and I submitted to her authority. Was one of us "better than" the other? Nope. Was one of us perfect or always right? No. In the world of pharmacy, authority is about who has been granted the position of authority by our company, who is recognized as the Pharmacist in Charge by the board of pharmacy of our state, and who carries the accountability of making the decisions.

It is exactly the same in marriage. The husband has authority only because God has assigned it to him to accomplish God's purposes of bringing glory to Himself. Husbands are not more intelligent, more capable, or "better than" wives. Men are not better than women. Women are not better than men. We are different, yet we have equal value before God. God has simply assigned husbands to sit in the driver's seat. If I try to drive from the passenger's seat, unless it is a real emergency and my husband is unconscious or incapacitated, I am likely to wreck the car, even if I am an amazing driver myself.

God has many great purposes in His design for marriage—authority, submission, love, and respect. He intends a godly marriage to draw many people to Christ outside of the family. He intends our marriages to display the very heart of the gospel to the world. He intends especially for a biblical marriage to draw the couple's children to Himself. He also intends a godly marriage to be the strong building block of society and churches—to protect morals, to teach virtues, to prepare the next generation to be responsible, mature, and godly men and women who know what masculinity, femininity, authority, submission, God, the Bible, marriage, and family are all about. God's design for marriage helps to produce a new godly generation. This is why God says He hates divorce, because it does not produce godly offspring (Mal. 2:15–16).

God intends to use a wife's submission to her husband as a constant example to children of how they are to submit to those in authority over them and to God. He wants to use a husband's constant example of Christ's strong, humble, loving, servant-hearted, sacrificial leadership to show children the character of God so they can relate to, love, and trust God. God desires to use a father's godly example of masculinity to show sons how to be godly husbands and fathers and to show daughters how to expect to be treated in their future marriages. God wants to use a mother's godly example to show her sons what to expect from their wives in the future and to demonstrate to her daughters how to be godly women, wives, and mothers. But biblical submission does far more than bless children, church, and country. It has practical blessings for us in our own marriages and in our own relationships with Christ as well.

Submission demonstrates trust.

Biblical submission to any God-given human authority is primarily about my respecting, reverencing, honoring, and trusting God in His sovereignty, and it is about my willingness to live in obedience and submission to Him. It has very little to do with the person to whom I am submitting. In fact, I could easily replace the word "submit" with the word "trust." Do I trust God? Am I willing to follow Him no matter what? The little details and individual decisions we face in marriage often aren't that big of a deal in the grand scheme of things. Sometimes we try to make little issues more important than the marriage, or more important than our honoring and obeying Christ. Thankfully, we can rest in God's promise that "in all things God works for the good of those who love him, who have been called according to his purpose" (Rom. 8:28). Because God's promises are true, I can trust Him with my husband's decisions (unless my husband is asking me to sin or do something dangerous, in which case I cannot follow my husband in that area). I can respectfully share my desires, ideas, needs, emotions, concerns, and wisdom with my husband; then I have the freedom and power to trust God to work through my husband's leadership to do what is ultimately best for me, our family, and God's kingdom. Stop. Read that sentence again, please, my precious sister. This is powerful stuff. A wife's willingness to submit to her husband may be one of the biggest tests of her faith in Christ. It will often only be in looking back that I will see how God was working through my husband's decisions. So I can look forward with anticipation to all of the amazing things God has in store for me, as I trust Him to lead me through Greg.

> ## "A wife's willingness to submit to her husband may be one of the biggest tests of her faith in Christ."

My husband will sin and make mistakes sometimes. I will also sin and make mistakes sometimes. We both fall at times even though we know and love Christ. The goal is that God will make us more and more like Jesus, but we won't reach total perfection on this earth. We will both need grace, forgiveness, and mercy from one another. It takes time for a man to learn to be a godly leader, just like it takes time for a woman to learn to be a godly follower. One decision is not a true measure of my husband's leadership. I can be patient as God works in my husband to help him learn from his mistakes, and he will grow as a leader, especially if I can continue to support him even in those difficult times. If I turn on Greg, give him the third degree, and heap contempt upon him, my husband may just become paralyzed and stop trying to lead. My Spirit-empowered response when my husband's decision doesn't turn out the way he had hoped is critical to inspire him to become a better leader. If I can support him, respect the good in him, stand with him, show faith in him, continue to trust him whenever possible and not take over, my husband will probably get back up and learn and become a stronger man of God.

From a Husband

Ultimately it all boils down to trust. . . . When a wife makes it clear that she trusts you—the next time you make a decision, you try to not gamble on it. You make sure it's the best deci-sion. You make sure to reward her trust.

Submission allows God to work.

My obedience to God opens up doors for Him to move in my life in ways that He cannot and will not when I am walking in disobedience to Him. Interestingly, as a wife is filled with God's peace, with great faith in Christ and total trust in Him, she is best able to demonstrate real trust in her husband as well. Men long to be trusted. Husbands tend to eventually respond to a wife's radiant faith by becoming bet-ter, more responsible, more trustworthy men. As a husband feels the weight of his wife's beautiful feminine trust, faith, admiration, and cooperation with his leadership, he is most encouraged and motivated to become more and more the man God calls him to be. This approach is so much more powerful than a worldly approach of nagging, crit-icizing, condemning, and preaching. A wife's obedience to God mo-tivates her husband like nothing else can to open his heart to want to hear and obey God. I don't control my husband. I let God change me and allow the changes God makes in me inspire my husband. I trust God to change my husband. When one spouse begins to obey God, He often opens the door, in time, for the other spouse to begin to desire to obey Him as well, which eventually opens the door to healing for the marriage.

What many wives don't realize is that we don't lose power and influ-ence when we obey God's Word and His commands for us as wives. The only power we lose is our sinful power to destroy, tear down, and harm. We gain the power of heaven! We gain the power of Christ! When we walk with Jesus and seek His glory above all else, we align ourselves with God's will and His desire to fulfill His conditional promises to us. E. M. Bounds writes, "Obedience can ask with boldness at the throne of grace, and those who are obedient are the only ones who can ask in that way."[7] When Christ is our Greatest Treasure, and we are able to hold everything but Christ loosely, we get to experience His power, His promises, and His miracles that we would otherwise forfeit. God does not guarantee us that we will get what we want when we obey Him. He does not guarantee to change our husbands. He does not guarantee to use our timetable. He does, however, guarantee that He will accomplish His will in our lives. He will change us and our desires. If we desire our husbands to become godly men, this is God's path for us. Then we leave the results to Him.

> If I had cherished sin in my heart, the Lord would not have listened. (Ps. 66:18)

From a Wife

My husband said [when I trust him in the small things, it] means the world to him. He feels that I trust his judgment, which causes him to want to make the best decision, so it causes him to really rely on the Lord for guidance, because my trust is something he does not want to lose. It makes him feel more competent and confident. My husband said [that when his wife argues constantly and doesn't cooperate with him, it makes him] feel like he can't do anything right. Not only does his wife not trust his judgment but he begins to second-guess himself and becomes paralyzed in his leadership. . . . He said when I used to behave like this, he felt that he wasn't needed, that he wasn't man enough or strong enough for me, and maybe he wasn't even the man for me. I never knew I was doing this much damage. . . . My husband said something very interesting, "I married a woman, but if a wife is constantly fighting for the position as head even over small things, it feels very competitive and like being married to a man."

Submission promotes real romance.

I want to be careful with this topic because I know that for many of us romance can easily become an idol. Paradoxically, if a woman seeks romance above all else, she will destroy any chance of having romance with her husband and her insatiable desire for romance will destroy the intimacy in her marriage. Idolatry always leads to our own destruction. It is only when Christ is in His proper place that we can experience God's best in every way for our lives, which often includes an increase in romance, sexual desire, and passion as each spouse embraces his or her God-designed role.

Control and aggression kill romance for both men and women. Passivity also kills romance on either side of the marriage. When we give each other space and time to give freely to one other without pressure, and when we seek to meet the other person's deepest God-given masculine or feminine needs, then romance may begin to grow. There is nothing romantic about a wife desperately trying to force her husband to be with her. There is also nothing romantic about a husband being passive, uninvolved in the family, and parked in front of the TV. Of course, there is not much to get excited about when a wife is a doormat or a husband is being a cruel tyrant, either. I find it interesting that when we are following God's pattern for male headship and female submission, conditions are the most favorable for us to have healthy marriages. When a wife focuses on the God-given differences between her own femininity and her husband's masculinity, these things can create incredible attraction and chemistry.

There is something wonderful about a husband choosing on his own to invite his wife to slow dance with him in the kitchen, saying, "I love you, baby. You're the most amazing woman I have ever met." There is something so fulfilling about a husband putting his arms around his wife's waist at the bathroom sink and kissing her neck just because he wants to, or winking at her from across the room with that twinkle in his eye because he feels his genuine masculinity so powerfully as he encounters her inspiring femininity. When a wife approaches her husband in a feminine, receptive, non-threatening way, her husband can better see his wife as his equal partner, not his competition. When he knows she trusts and honors him and that he is safe with her, he will likely be drawn to her demonstration of godly femininity. When a wife views her husband as strong and masculine, and recognizes the good that is in him, she is likely to feel a powerful pull of attraction toward her husband. Godliness is very attractive in our spouses! So many times, intimacy in marriage increases—at least in some ways—after one spouse devotes herself or himself fully to Christ. Sometimes this takes many years, maybe decades. But even if a spouse never changes, being close to Christ and experiencing His Spirit transforming one's life is more than worth it.

How One Husband Feels When His Wife Trusts Him to Lead

[If she belongs to me and allows me to shepherd and care for her] then I feel responsible to help her. I have to be her oak under which she finds shelter and help her weather her storms. If she doesn't [act like she belongs to me] then I feel irritated and annoyed that she is coming to me with her problems. . . . If she doesn't look to me as her leader then she can find her own happiness and I'll find mine. If she does . . . like belonging to me, then the lengths to which I would go to make her happy are going to far exceed those of which she will ever go for me. This, in my limited understanding, is how Christ loves us. If we choose to belong to Him and accept His lead, He will show us more love than we can understand. If we refuse Him and demand to be in charge, then we have no promise.

A Husband Shares About Dependency in Marriage

Of course your husband is not superior to you—neither is your boss. Your husband is above you, not superior. There's a difference. That means he may give directives and you can choose to obey them or not. If you submit to him, then he knows that he's responsible for the things he asks of you. He will be held accountable unless what he asks you is a sin and you knowingly do it. What I mean is—yes, you're equal in value, but not in roles. He plays the role of leading you and you follow. He cannot play his role unless you play yours. He cannot defend you if you defend yourself. He cannot provide for you if you provide for yourself. Basically, independence weakens relationships but [healthy] dependence strengthens them. Once . . . you can trust God, what on earth can your husband do to harm you? Your husband is a just a man, but God is everything.

This husband has an important point. We value independence so much in our culture today. We teach women to be totally self-sufficient so that they "don't need a man." Certainly there are times when it is necessary for us to be self-sufficient in some ways. If a husband becomes very ill, has to go away for a long deployment, leaves her, or dies, a wife may need the skills to be able to provide for herself, to make her own decisions, to handle her finances alone, and so on. However, it is possible in a marriage for us to become too independent. Marriage is about the two becoming one. A spouse's spirit of independence can tear the marriage relationship apart.

There is a level of interdependence that is needed in a marriage relationship, where both spouses realize they are part of a team and they are both contributing to making the other stronger than either one of them could be on his or her own. "We" becomes more important in marriage than "I." Of course, a wife may also become so dependent on her husband that she becomes "enmeshed" or "codependent," trying to be responsible for her husband and making him responsible for her. That is not God's design either. We must use caution here and continue to keep Christ as the focus of our life.

> "There is a level of interdependence that is needed in a marriage relationship, where both spouses realize they are part of a team and they are both contributing to making the other stronger than either one of them could be on his or her own."

Ultimately all of our faith, trust, and hope are in Him alone. Then we can be totally dependent on Christ and we will be neither too independent nor codependent, but instead interdependent in our marriages.

> Lord,
> Help me to fully understand and submit to Your beautiful design for marriage. Make me into a good gift for my husband! Use our marriage to bless other people and to attract many to Christ.
> Let my life bring You great glory and honor, however You see fit. I am fully Yours. Make me like Jesus and use me for Your kingdom. I yield myself completely to You. I trust You no matter what happens, Lord!
> If I have You, I will be content. You are all I need. You are my very great reward, my shield, and my treasure. Nothing can rob me of the peace, joy, and abundant spiritual life You have given me.
> In the name and power of Jesus my Lord, amen!

6

Recognizing Disrespect

There is a whole world of masculine respect that I knew nothing about for most of my life. When God began to open my eyes to all of this, I was in absolute awe of what I had missed for so long. How could I not have seen this? Men have an entirely different way of looking at life, a different paradigm, a different way of processing emotions, a different way of thinking, and a different way of speaking than women do. Masculinity almost seemed like an alternate reality when I first began to explore it.

Of course, each individual man has his own unique perspective, personality, strengths, emotions, and method of processing decisions, as well. After my wake-up call from *Love and Respect* by Dr. Emerson Eggerichs, I asked Greg to tell me what was respectful and disrespectful to him. I thought he would just take about five minutes, I would write down a few things in each column, and I would be ready to be a godly wife. Problem solved. I was shocked and confused when he said sincerely, "I don't really know." That made this process much more difficult as I tried to figure out respect and disrespect on my own.

There are a lot of words and actions that can feel disrespectful (or unloving) to men, just as there are a lot of words and actions that can feel unloving (or disrespectful) to women. Some of these are universally disrespectful to all men regardless of culture and personality; others are more about individual perception and preferences. It is important for each woman to study her own husband to learn what he feels is disrespectful. It is also important to be able to distinguish that there are a few husbands who have unreasonable expectations. Men are sinners just like women. It is possible for husbands to idolize feeling respected just like some wives idolize feeling loved. When that is the case, it is good for a woman to remember that she is ultimately seeking to please God, not her husband. Women must seek God's wisdom to navigate this tricky boundary line.

Many of the things that husbands say make them feel disrespected may at first seem insignificant to us as women. We may even feel that avoiding some of these behaviors may be impossible and that men should "just get over themselves," as one of my readers put it. I am here to tell you, my precious sister in Christ, that it is indeed possible to cut out intentional—and eventually unintentional—disrespect and to learn to speak this strange new language of respect pretty fluently. It takes much prayer, dying to self, study, practice, input from your husband, and the Holy Spirit's power working in you, but it is absolutely possible in time.*

One of the greatest temptations early in this journey will be for you to want to learn to respect your husband in order to try to change him, to make him be more loving, or to get what you want from him. That won't work. Husbands know when our motives are selfish; God knows,

---

*Remember, if your husband is involved in unrepentant infidelity, is abusive to you or your children, has active addictions to drugs or alcohol, has an extreme addiction to pornography, is involved in criminal activities, or has mental health disorders, please seek appropriate help. You may need godly, experienced, mature, wise help to navigate your marriage wisely. I am not referring to these types of situations as I share about what husbands need.

too! You want your husband to love you because he really loves you, not because he wants something from you. Husbands feel the same way about us respecting them. I am not talking about pretending, being fake, and playing games. I am talking about total heart change, which is a very long process. We will leave the results and the timing of what happens in our husbands' lives up to God in His amazing sovereignty, as we seek to allow God to transform *us*.

> "One of the greatest temptations early in this journey will be for you to want to learn to respect your husband in order to try to change him, to make him be more loving, or to get what you want from him. That won't work."

Lord,

I pray that You might give me insights into my husband's heart, mind, and soul. Help me to be receptive to anything You want to place Your finger on in my life. Help me to resist feelings of defensiveness or a desire to write a list of all the things that my husband does that make me feel unloved. I know that You know the ways my husband hurts me and that You will deal with him about those issues. I trust You with any pain I carry. I am not seeking to change to be what my husband wants me to be. My goal is to become the woman You desire me to be.

In the name and power of Christ, amen.

What Speaks Disrespect to Husbands

This list of words and actions that husbands may find disrespectful was compiled from a number of different husbands. Please don't think of this as a list of don'ts or a list of rules, but rather as a way of learning whether you may be unintentionally communicating disrespect to your husband and how to better speak his language. Your husband probably won't agree with everything that is on this list. He has his own ideas that are more important than what other husbands have shared. If he is willing to share the things that most speak disrespect to him, go with his list, not mine! If you are ready to hear your husband's heart without defending yourself, perhaps you'd like to ask your husband to look at this list and check the things that feel disrespectful to him. Then you can focus only on the issues that matter to him.

These are words and actions that can sometimes wound or anger a husband and make him feel unloved, disrespected, and unvalued, even if the pain is unintentional. You are welcome to put a check beside the things that you think might be issues for you:

____ Implying that he is not intelligent, capable, or competent

____ Implying, even slightly, that he is not enough for you sexually or that sex with him is not fulfilling to you

____ Implying that you see yourself as being spiritually or morally superior to him

____ Giving him directives, demands, or orders; telling him what to do; or bossing him around. "You should . . . ," "You'd better . . . ," "You need to . . . ," "I want you to . . . "

____ Questioning his decisions, particularly with the word "why?" For many men, saying, "Why would you . . . ?" implies that we think they are "stupid." The wording is the issue here, not the sincere questions, usually.

____ Questioning everything he does. Sometimes just the sheer volume of questions can be an issue.

____ Telling other people he is one of your children or treating him like a child

____ Trying to control him or make decisions for him

____ Comparing him unfavorably to another man

___ Putting him down, criticizing him, belittling him, making
   fun of him, mocking him, or insulting him at any time, but
   especially in front of others
___ Using body language that communicates contempt, hatred,
   or condemnation, such as rolling your eyes, speaking in an
   angry tone of voice, giving "the angry mama look," sighing, or
   putting your hands on your hips
___ Implying that he is not a good father
___ Being unhappy most of the time. A husband often feels like a
   failure as a man, husband, and dad if his wife is not happy.
___ Undermining his authority as a father, especially in front of
   your children, by telling your children they don't have to do
   what their dad said to do (unless he is asking them to sin or
   to do something truly dangerous and you don't have time to
   speak privately about it with him)
___ Trying to help him "too much," especially when he didn't ask
   for help
___ Interrupting him (unless there is an emergency)
___ Purposely ignoring him
___ Correcting his manners, especially in front of other people
___ Not having faith in him when he is responsible
___ Not trusting him when he is trustworthy
___ Not caring about his feelings or opinions
___ Using sarcasm to tear him down
___ Putting other things or people above him on your priority list:
   children, extended family, friends, church, or ministry
___ Being overly afraid of him
___ Taking him for granted
___ Idolizing him as more important than God in your life
___ Being constantly disappointed that he can't meet your deepest
   spiritual needs that only Jesus can meet
___ Having impossibly high and unrealistic expectations of him

____ Answering for him

____ Having an entitlement mentality that "he owes me"

____ Bringing up his sins and mistakes of the past that you said you forgave him for already

____ Gossiping about him

____ Not sharing your ideas, thoughts, concerns, and opinions with him

____ Trying to change him instead of accepting him as he is

____ Refusing to accept his answer and continuing to question him

____ Asking, "Are you sure?" after he has given a confident *yes* already

____ Saying, "Do you know what you are doing?" (There are more respectful ways to voice our concerns.)

____ Telling him how to drive, how to fix something, how to do his job, how to manage the children, how to dress, how to eat. He wants a wife and partner, not a mother.

____ Arguing with him, especially in front of the children or other people. But even arguing in private is disrespectful. God actually commands us as believers not to argue or complain (Phil. 2:14–16).

____ Making light of something he thinks is important

____ Correcting him when he is telling stories to other people (especially on very minor details that don't ultimately matter much)

____ Snooping and spying on him on his phone, Facebook, or email (Ideally, you would both be totally open about these things. If you really believe he is being unfaithful or lying about something major, perhaps it may seem worth it to investigate, but keep in mind that if he is not doing something wrong, you may damage his trust in you by spying on him. Maybe there could be another way to approach the situation. It could be something to pray about and for which to seek wise, godly counsel.)

____ Apologizing but then justifying or explaining yourself
____ Complaining
____ Nagging
____ Assuming he is wrong if he disagrees with you
____ Withholding sex or rejecting him sexually
____ Attempting to force sex on him when he is feeling disrespected
     or exhausted or has a medical issue
____ Demanding his time, his attention, his affection, or sex
____ Demanding that he do something right now (unless there is
     an emergency)
____ Doing something loving or respectful for him and expecting
     him to do something specific in return

It should go without saying that anything that is extremely disrespectful has no place in *any* relationship, marital or otherwise. The
majority of the following are unquestionably sinful. But, here's the list
anyway:

____ Screaming
____ Name-calling
____ Assassinating his character
____ Cursing
____ Publically humiliating him on social media or in front of
     others
____ Making threats of physical harm
____ Throwing things
____ Insulting his masculinity
____ Threatening to have an affair
____ Flirting with other men
____ Accusing him of having an affair, without clear evidence
____ Using sex as a weapon or as a way to get him to give you
     things you want

____ Hitting, slapping, punching, pushing, or grabbing a weapon (This is *never* okay for anyone to do to someone else! Please seek godly, experienced help right away if you are physically abusing or threatening to physically abuse your husband or anyone else. If you or your children are not safe, please get help ASAP!)

____ Putting all of his belongings outside

____ Following him around town

____ Lying

____ Teaching his children to disrespect or hate him

____ Threatening to leave or to divorce him

____ Shaming him for coming to you with his sexual needs

Whether our disrespect is intentional or not, these kinds of actions, words, and attitudes can deeply wound and repel our men. Our respect encourages and inspires our men to become the men God desires them to be. They may not, in our minds, deserve respect all the time. But the same God who commands us to unconditionally respect our husbands and honor their leadership also commands husbands to love their wives unconditionally. God definitely knew what He was talking about when He instructed husbands to love us unconditionally. I have learned that He knows exactly what He is talking about when it comes to what husbands need, too.

> "I need my husband's love
> even when I don't deserve it, in
> exactly the same way that my
> husband needs my respect even
> when he doesn't deserve it."

As husbands and wives seek to obey God's commands in marriage, we are forced to stretch, grow, depend on God, and become more holy.

That is God's desire. It helps me to remember that I need my husband's love even when I don't deserve it, in exactly the same way that my husband needs my respect even when he doesn't deserve it.

A Husband Shares His Heart

A woman who disrespects her husband pours out hate upon him. It won't be long until he is broken. A woman who respects her husband pours out love upon him. It won't be long until he is trying to conquer the world for her.

THE PERVASIVENESS OF DISRESPECT

As you observe the interactions of men and women this coming week in real life and on TV, be on the lookout for ways that women might treat men with disrespect. See if you notice the subtle ways that men respond when they feel disrespected by women. Watch for the clenched jaw, the nervous movements, the sudden countenance change, the "anger that comes out of nowhere," or the way a man quickly unplugs or leaves.

Once you realize what disrespect is, you will see it everywhere. It is kind of shocking. You'll see it when a young couple is walking somewhere and the wife says to her man with disdain in her voice, "Why would you go *that* way?" You'll see disrespect when a couple is shopping at the grocery store and the wife begins to loudly humiliate her husband about something and he suddenly walks away while she continues screaming at him about what a loser he is. You'll see disrespect when a dear friend of yours cuts her husband down with sarcasm in front of you and your soul will be pierced and later haunted by the hurt in his eyes. You may even see the results of your own disrespect when something flies out of your mouth before you had a chance to think about it and you see the way your husband looks at you. You'll want to erase every word.

Kayla's Demon

From my friend, Kayla, a story that took place one month into her journey:

> Wednesday was just an ordinary day until my husband got home from work. We haven't been sleeping very well, and he's been tired. So he sat down in the chair and turned on the TV while I started fixing supper. One little thing like the TV being on quickly invites my demon (yes, I believe everyone has a demon that studies them and tempts them constantly) into a conversation with me. The demon says, "You're headed right back to the life where you only speak to your husband [during] commercials. Even re-runs are more important than you and the kids." I know my Savior. I can feel the Holy Spirit move. However, I don't hear from God like I hear from my demon. I can pray and spend time in silence after begging God to speak, and feel like after a day of fasting, I still am clueless what God is saying to me, or if He is speaking at all. But the very moment something pulls on my frustrations, fears, insecurities, or weaknesses, I can hear so vividly and clearly the voice of my demon and am able to carry on long detailed conversations. This time when my demon started talking to me, I spoke back, but not in my normal fashion. I said, "Get behind me Satan. I'm not going down this road anymore." My husband left to go play guitar. He's been doing this once a week after the kids go to bed and I love it! It gets him out of the house, he has the chance to play and grow in his talent, and I have plenty of time to play around on the computer, crochet, or do anything I want without the guilt of ignoring him or the kids. When my husband left, my demon started talking to me again. "He was tired tonight, but he has enough energy to go play guitar and stay out till midnight?" For 11 years, I took the bait and would

spin totally out of control. I'd spend hours at a time ripping my husband to shreds to myself because I let my sinful self decide where the conversation went.

In the last month, God has been teaching me things and exposing my sins in grave detail in a way I've been so blind to in the past. This time, I took those temptations to rip my husband apart and I purposely did the opposite. I sent my husband a text thanking him for folding the clothes. How could I almost have missed that he did that for me? I spent time praying for him and thinking about how much we've grown in our marriage. When he got home, I was already in bed. I usually stayed up waiting for him to get home. When he came to bed, he turned on the TV. I know, I know, the stinking TV is the center of my Wednesday! We fought quite a few times, jokingly and in some very heated and hurtful conversations about the TV at night. I like total darkness and complete silence. He likes the TV to be on. I bet you know what happened. My demon whispered so tenderly to my ears it practically gave me chills down my neck. "How come for 11 years *he* is the one who always gets to go to bed the way he prefers? Why did he automatically decide you have to learn to go to sleep with the TV on? Why can't he learn to go to sleep with it off?"

I was so afraid of what I might do next. I kissed my husband on the cheek, said, "I love you," and then told him I was going to go ahead and sleep on the couch. When he asked why, I just said as respectfully as I could, "I can't sleep in here tonight." I had to remove myself. Do you have any idea how many times we've fought while trying to go to bed because I've had hours of husband-bashing sessions with my demon and then I take the opportunity to tear him apart to his face for how awful he is, how badly he messes up, and how much he hurts me?

I settled down on the couch and quickly heard, "Why isn't

he out here? He knows the TV is bugging you. Why isn't he saying you should jump back in bed and he'll sleep on the couch? Oh yeah, and don't forget about this: even though you told him you really need it, he still isn't praying with you." Ouch. The most tender point of devastation and he had to go there. My demon knows me so well. The TV has nothing to do with praying together, and he brought it up as a last resort to get me to give in to my sinful desires, walk back in that room, and destroy the intimacy, respect, trust, and unity in our marriage.

I prayed and I told my demon that I have so much sin of my own and I am called to respect my husband no matter what I think or feel in any given moment. I purposefully for the very first time in my life took my thoughts captive, stopped the demon from talking to me, and went to sleep. I woke up so relieved! I didn't say a bunch of really mean or hurtful things I couldn't take back. I kept the TV in perspective and didn't allow that to be the standard by which I measured him as a husband and father. I took my thoughts captive and spoke truth over the lies.

I can do this with the help the Holy Spirit is providing. These boulders can be moved and these habits can be changed. There are two main reasons why I am finally finding freedom and success. And they have nothing to do with who my husband is, how he acts, or how he treats me. (Because, ladies, I got a really good one.)

Kayla went on to explain two really key points that we all need to remember. First, we are not better than our husbands. You may not have the particular sin struggle that your husband does, but you still have sin in your life at times, too. Second, we are going to answer for our own sins before God, not our husbands' sins. God requires obedience under any circumstances. When we notice ourselves meditating on many accusations against our husbands, it may be wise for us to question whether we might be listening to Satan, who is called "the accuser." Thankfully, as we learn to examine each thought that pops into our minds by the truth of Scripture and as we submit to God's Spirit, we can learn to recognize the voice of the enemy and we can learn to hear God's still, small voice much more clearly. Spending time daily in the Bible and in deep prayer as we seek God with all our hearts gives us His Spirit's power to hear and to obey Him.

> "First, we are not better than our husbands. . . . Second, we are going to answer for our own sins before God, not our husbands' sins."

Anyone who does not enter the sheep pen by the gate, but climbs in by some other way, is a thief and a robber. The one who enters by the gate is the shepherd of the sheep. . . . He calls his own sheep by name and leads them out . . . and his sheep follow him because they know his voice. But they will never follow a stranger; in fact, they will run away from him because they do not recognize a stranger's voice. (John 10:1–5)

The Voice in His Head—by Greg

April asked me about whether a guy has similar voices in his head that paint a bad picture of his wife's intentions. I told her that I do have a voice in my head, but it rarely talks about her. It is a voice telling me things like, "You don't have what it takes to do _____," "You are a failure at _____," "You are an inadequate husband, father, or son," and, "You are not good enough." Now, I need to clarify that this voice isn't on all of the time, and it is usually confined to one topic at a time. This is very different from what April explained to me about how she had an internal voice accusing me and justifying her disrespect and need for control almost constantly earlier in our marriage just like what Kayla described in the last story. [It might be interesting to ask your husband if he can relate to Greg's experience here.]

Most wives want their husbands to be the godly leaders of their families. Most husbands want their wives to be their biggest supporters and encouragers. When a husband can feel that he has his wife's trust and appreciation, it is like giving him a shot of energy. That is why it is so easy for a man to become unplugged when he does not feel he is getting this support. I know there are many who might say, "My husband is definitely not the godly leader in our family and there is no way I can affirm him after what he has done." Unfortunately, these husbands probably need the most support from their wives. If we understand that Satan's plan is to attack our marriages and families, maybe we can start silencing the voices. I know when I feel that my wife is in full support with me about something, the voice I hear is, "You can do this because she trusts and believes in you."

MOVING FORWARD

Some women may relate to Greg's thoughts above. There are many who attack and loathe themselves and are crippled with fear, guilt, shame, and feelings of worthlessness. There are some husbands who cooperate with Satan to heap accusation against their wives, as well. These destructive voices are an attack from the enemy and our sinful flesh. Let's recognize his strategies to destroy us and stop listening to him, seeking only to hear God's voice and to embrace God's truth.

"Marriage teaches us much about
our relationship with Christ. And
our relationship with Christ teaches
us much about marriage."

This is what I long for for all of us in our marriages: that we would stop unwittingly cooperating with the enemy, that we would unite forces with our respective husbands and God, and that we would experience God's victory, blessings, and glory in our marriages. We have so much power to either destroy or build up our men with our words, attitudes, and actions. As we get rid of disrespect, even unintentional disrespect, we take a big step forward in better understanding our husbands and their masculine needs. We also become more and more the godly women Jesus desires us to be. Marriage teaches us much about our relationship with Christ. And our relationship with Christ teaches us much about marriage.

> *Lord,*
> *I lift up myself, my husband, and my marriage to You. Thank You that You are able to heal me and restore me. Thank You for Your forgiveness, mercy, and grace. Help me not to be overcome by worldly sorrow that leads to death, but if I need to repent of something, grant me godly sorrow that leads to a changed life in Christ. Help me to better understand my husband and masculinity. Give me Your eyes, Your heart, Your love, and Your mind as I seek to love my husband as You do. Change my heart's desires to match Your own. I love and trust You, Jesus!*
> *In the name and power of Christ, amen!*

Acknowledging Our Sin

Maybe you are beginning to realize now that you have deeply wounded your husband and caused damage to the unity of your marriage by sinning against him and God with your disrespect and attempts to control him. This realization can be overwhelming. Or if you have been overly quiet and passive, maybe you are beginning to realize that you have not been contributing enough to the decisions in your marriage and that your husband may need to hear more of your feminine voice and godly influence. Maybe you have not had an issue with disrespect in your marriage at all. If so, that is wonderful! Perhaps God is formulating ways for you to articulate what being a godly wife means to struggling wives, and maybe God is developing your heart to minister to wives who are hurting. For those who now see sin in their lives, there is every reason for hope in Christ! I don't want anyone to ever be discouraged.

Godly sorrow brings repentance that leads to salvation and leaves no regret, but worldly sorrow brings death. (2 Cor. 7:10)

REPENT BEFORE GOD

God is holy and completely good. He alone has the authority and right to determine what is wrong and what is right. Repent to God for all the sins you can think of. This means we completely abandon anything God calls "sin" or "wrong" and we run toward Him with all that is in us. I personally needed to write everything down that God brought to my mind from the course of our marriage and turn from each thing individually. At first, I had many things to write down every day for about six weeks. This is part of an ongoing habit of daily repentance of anything we have done that may offend God. We turn away from every ungodly thought, every trace of bitterness, every bit of unforgiveness, every hint of having a critical spirit, every bit of pride, self-loathing, lies, thinking we are better than someone else, hatred, unbelief, and every shred of disrespect for God. We turn away from disrespect for husbands, flirtations with other men, fear, worry, and worldly guilt.

> "God is holy and completely good.
> He alone has the authority
> and right to determine what is
> wrong and what is right."

This turning away involves examining all of your motives, hidden thoughts, and desires, allowing God to expose anything that offends Him. Be still and allow His Word and His Spirit access and freedom to examine the darkest corners of your soul. This part is painful, ladies! But don't give up; it is more than worth it! God will often reveal your sin to you in layers over time. It may be years before you see all of the layers. Ask Him to show you every sin, to help you to repent, to turn completely away from all your sin, and turn fully to Christ for forgiveness, new life, and the power of His Spirit. If there is something God has impressed on your heart that He desires you to repent from,

I would recommend reading Psalm 51 during your quiet time one day this week and journaling about your response to the three verses that speak most to you.

I used to think that I could never love God as much as people who were forgiven for "big sins" when I read what Jesus said about the woman who poured expensive perfume on Jesus's feet and wiped his feet with her hair: "Her many sins have been forgiven—as her great love has shown. But whoever has been forgiven little loves little" (Luke 7:47). But when God showed me the depth of my sin, I finally realized that I, too, have been forgiven *much*. This has allowed me to love Jesus more than I ever have before in my life! We are all in need of great forgiveness for we all have many, many sins.

> *Lord,*
> *Please give me wisdom about the next steps to take. Thank You that Your blood can cleanse me and make my heart "as white as snow" (Isa. 1:18). Thank You that real love and real life are available to me through Jesus's death on the cross on my behalf. Give me a tender, receptive heart to You. Give me strength and grace to bear any response my husband may have to my changing heart. Show me how to make things right with you and my husband.*
> *In the name of Christ, amen!*

APOLOGIZE TO YOUR HUSBAND

I offer you no rules for apologizing to your husband, simply ideas to prayerfully consider as you listen for God's Spirit to speak His wisdom to your heart. I would love for you to spend a good bit of time in prayer before deciding how to approach your husband, maybe even several days or weeks. If you do believe God desires you to apologize for something, please read the rest of this chapter before doing anything. You don't have to rush this. You may want to have time to think through your options and wait on God's prompting. Remember that God knows the specifics of your situation that I do not know. Sometimes God will prompt a wife not to verbally apologize because the husband is at a place where he doesn't value her words anymore. In that case, a wife may decide God is leading her to say nothing but to begin changing her attitude, words, heart, and behavior. Other wives will realize they do need to say something, but it is wise to choose our words carefully and prayerfully.

I would suggest apologizing in person if possible. Choose a time when your husband is calm, things are going fairly well, and you have time alone. Another idea is to email or write out your apology. A lot of men appreciate brevity. Think bullet points or think in terms of three to six sentences or so, unless you know that your husband likes deep, detailed, thorough discussions about this kind of thing. If he loves words, you may decide to be more verbose. Apologize once, generally. Multiple apologies are not usually necessary and can make it seem like you are not receiving your husband's forgiveness, if he offers it to you. It is really important *not* to justify or explain the reasons for your sin. When I say, "I apologize for doing X, but you did Y," it sounds like I believe I was right and my husband was more wrong than I was. This only adds more disrespect to the situation and negates my apology.

Please don't try to force him to forgive you. He is responsible for his own emotions, his behavior, his actions, his words, his sin, and his obedience to God. Realize he may need a few days, weeks, or months to process what you said. Some men need time to think about things before they can talk about them. Be gracious and receive his forgiveness if he offers it. Agree with him that you were wrong in those instances without getting defensive. It is not necessary to apologize for things that you did not do or to admit fault where you truly did nothing wrong. You do need to respect your husband, but you can also respect God and yourself by being truthful and not agreeing that you sinned if you really didn't sin.

Maybe you were not controlling and disrespectful, but rather too passive or too quiet. Maybe you were terribly afraid of upsetting your husband and just tried to please him no matter what the cost. Maybe you put your husband above God in your heart and valued your husband's approval more than God's. Maybe you have not learned how to use your ideas, influence, personality, gifts, talents, intelligence, and femininity to bless your husband and family. In that case, spend some time in prayer and in God's Word and seek His wisdom about the next steps to take.

Does God want you to verbally apologize to your husband, or does He want you to just begin to change as you seek to become the woman He calls you to be? Perhaps you only need to repent to God if you have sinned against Him in some way. It will depend upon your situation. If you know Christ, God can impress upon your heart exactly what He wants you to do or say to begin to make things right with your husband.

If you are apologizing for being too quiet, you may just want to say something simple like,

> Honey, I see now that I have not been as involved and plugged into our marriage as I really should be. I want to change. I want to begin to share my ideas and opinions more, even though that can be really challenging for me sometimes. I would greatly appreciate your encouragement and support as I seek to become more of the wife God desires me to be.

If your husband is a believer in Christ, here is one example of the kinds of things God may inspire you to say if you are apologizing for control and disrespect:

> Honey, I'm so thankful that you are my husband. I am afraid I haven't always shown you appreciation like I should have. I can see now that I have been disrespectful, controlling, and

contentious sometimes. I have fought against your God-given leadership in our marriage. I was wrong. I am *so* very sorry! I want to learn to be a godly wife. I want to learn to properly respect you, to honor God, and to honor your leadership in our marriage. I hope you can forgive me and be patient with me as I unlearn everything I thought I knew and start from scratch with all of this. I have a very long way to go on this journey.

I hope you will feel free to tell me when I come across disrespectfully because I know I don't really "get" what is disrespectful and what is respectful yet, and I want to learn. I appreciate your wisdom and patience as I try to understand your needs and how you think. I care about your feelings, your perspective, and the things that are important to you.

You have my full support and trust as the head of our family from this moment on as I seek to learn to follow you well. This is all new to me, but I want you to feel like the most respected husband in the world one day!

And you are done apologizing! Now comes the hard part of actually relinquishing control of your husband and the marriage and stopping intentional and unintentional disrespect in everyday life.

If your husband is not a believer in Christ, follow Scripture's command for wives in this situation and do not talk about God or spiritual things (1 Peter 3:1–2). Here is one possible example of how a wife may handle this kind of situation if she needs to apologize for disrespect and control:

Babe, I am so thankful that you are in my life. I'm not sure I have always shown my appreciation for you the way I should have. I realize that I have been disrespectful, controlling, and argumentative toward you. I was wrong. I am *so* very sorry! It stressed me out a lot trying to "be the man" in our marriage.

I'm stepping down now. I want you to know that I trust you and I support your leadership. I have a lot to learn. I feel pretty clueless about how to completely change my thinking, but I want to do this and to be a great wife to you, no matter how long it takes me to really "get it." I am open to hearing anything you want to share with me about how you feel and what you need from me.

Your Husband's Response

There are a lot of ways that a husband might respond to an apology—as many ways as there are husbands, no doubt. But here we'll look at some common responses.

Silence

After an apology, your husband may be totally quiet. My suggestion is to wait patiently a few minutes. Don't stare at him. Maybe sit shoulder-to-shoulder with him. Don't pressure him or try to make him respond by a certain time. If he doesn't say anything, eventually thank him for listening. He doesn't have to say anything. This is about you seeking to make things right on your end. Hug and kiss him if he is receptive, and move on into a new chapter of learning to be a godly wife. It may take your man time to process this. He will be carefully watching your behavior and attitude for months, maybe even years, to see if you are for real. Words often don't mean a lot to men. Actions are what speak most forcefully to them.

Reluctance

He may say he doesn't want to lead. That's fine—no need to argue! Just wait on him and continue to step down and allow him to have the time and space he needs to begin to step up. It may be a gradual process of releasing control a little bit at a time, if that is what God leads you to do, rather than dropping everything in your husband's lap at once. As your husband sees he is safe and that you will actually honor his leadership, he will grow in confidence and eventually may begin to try to lead. He may have a lot of learning to do, especially if he never led before and he didn't have a godly example in his own father when he was growing up. He will need your patience, support, and grace to be willing to try this. No need to talk about it a lot. Just wait on him and look to him when it is time to make big decisions. Ask him what he wants to do. Be interested and responsive to his opinions and suggestions. If God gives you the green light, share your ideas, feelings, and needs, as well. If God prompts you to hold back your thoughts for a while, obey God's voice.

> "At first, a husband who is reluctant
> to lead may only give suggestions,
> but that may be the way he
> is trying to start to lead."

At first, a husband who is reluctant to lead may only give suggestions, but that may be the way he is trying to start to lead. Sometimes husbands who have been really passive are afraid of sounding like a selfish tyrant, so they try to use a very soft approach. It might even help for you to say, "I hear you giving me a suggestion. Is this actually just a suggestion, or is it something that is important to you, honey? It's okay if this is important to you. I want to understand you clearly." Smile. Give him time to think about things. Have a cooperative spirit. He will need room to mess up sometimes. You will need that kind of room, too. Becoming a godly wife usually takes years; it isn't a simple flip of a light switch.

Hurt

He may cry or share with you how wounded he has been because of your sin against him. A number of men I've encountered have felt so devastated by their wife's disrespect for them that they've actually been suicidal, but they never told their wife the depth of their pain. If your husband is upset, please listen. Hear him. Don't argue. Agree you were wrong in those instances where you were wrong. Empathize with his pain. Don't attack him. Don't make it about your hurt or about what he has done wrong. There will be an appropriate time to talk about your pain during a different conversation in the future. Don't defend yourself. Say something like, "I am terribly sorry for hurting you so much!" Or say, "I hear what you are saying." Or, "I think I understand," if you truly do understand his pain. You can also say something like, "Thank you so much for sharing all of this with me. I want to be a safe place for you from now on. I don't ever want to hurt you."

Anger

He may get angry and start listing all the ways he feels you have disrespected him. Please don't argue! Listen to him. He may tell you things that he feels you need to work on. Be open to hearing them. Take him and his concerns seriously. Write down what he is saying if you are not sure you will remember. He may finally feel free to tell you just how awful he has felt in the marriage for a long time because he thinks maybe now you finally get it. Then take his comments, concerns, complaints, and criticisms about you before God to prayerfully study and consider in light of God's Word. Are there any legitimate criticisms? Then, praise God for leading you through your husband, and ask God to help you change in any areas that you need to change. If there are some criticisms that are not justifiable in God's Word and that are truly unreasonable, let those go from your mind and heart. Sometimes people lash out with criticism when they are hurting. Evaluating whether the criticisms are valid or not will require God's wisdom and discernment.

Remember, you are not responsible *for* your husband. You are only responsible for you. You are responsible *to* your husband—to treat him well, as God asks you to. But you are not responsible for how he responds, his sin, his walk with Christ, or his emotions. Part of living by faith is that you step back and allow God to work on your husband. There is no guarantee. But you, from now on, can become more and more the woman God wants you to be. As you sin less and are more controlled by God's Spirit, your husband is much more likely to be drawn to God and to you. That is the way God designed things to be.

There is a confusing thing that can happen sometimes. Some husbands seem to become more unloving for a while. It could be because they feel free to have their own voice again for the first time. They may be testing their wife's sincerity. I suggest that you just keep on being the woman God calls you to be and don't let your husband's behavior tempt you into sinning against him. Just focus on Christ and obeying Him no matter what your husband does. If things get unbearable or abusive, please seek appropriate help.

> "Even if your husband never changes, we can trust our sovereign, holy God! God will change *us!*"

Another thing that can be a challenge is that when a wife changes a husband may not be able to blame his wife anymore for his sin against her. He may try to get her to go back to her old ways so that he doesn't have to face his own sin. Again, please keep pressing on toward Christ and keep doing what God calls you to do. This can get unpleasant sometimes when a husband is being convicted by God and isn't yet ready to face his guilt. But keep clinging to Christ, my sweet sister! Even if your husband never changes, we can trust our sovereign, holy God! God will change *us!* We must get to the point where we are willing to trust God regardless of results here on earth.

TESTIMONIES FROM PEACEFUL WIFE'S BLOG READERS

I'm so thankful for the wives who have allowed me to share their stories. As you contemplate your own apology to your husband, consider
what these women did. The support and encouragement of other godly
wives can be a great help as we pursue God's peace in our marriages.

Wife 1

When I apologized to my husband, we were laying in bed together, talking, laughing, and just enjoying time together. . . .
I told him a lot of things I appreciated about him—things he
did for me and general things that I loved about him. I told
him how thankful I was that he put up with me. He laughed
as if to say, "What are you talking about?" I named things I
did that were disrespectful, and shared how much conviction
I had that I was not obeying God. He looked at me in confusion and said, "Babe, what are you talking about? You are
fine. You are perfect. I love you." What? This is the same guy
I got in an argument with last week and he told me I was disrespecting him—and a few weeks ago he told me I was being
selfish. Before that he asked me why I was being a brat. I just
apologized and promised that I was going to try my hardest to
change and let him know I knew God was sovereign enough to
make me a godly wife if I was willing. He smiled, hugged me,
loved on me, and dropped it. I could tell by his actions that he
appreciated my apology.

The next day . . . I apologized again to him and let him
know that I need him, love him, respect him, and I want to
be there for him. I want to lift him up and be an awesome
helpmeet for him. . . . He then said that he was sorry. I was
confused. My husband explained that he was embarrassed
by my apologies. He was embarrassed that he had called me

disrespectful, bratty, and selfish—when all the while God was working on me and needed no help from him. He felt convicted that I felt convicted! It taught us both a big lesson about trusting our spouse to God. He said that all those times he was trying to force me to be more respectful he could have just loved me and let God handle the dirty work. Still, I am so glad I apologized. His response was humbling and reminded me to continue to trust him to the Lord. . . . The strength I get from God is so tangible I can feel Him cheering me along sometimes. My marriage is better than ever. I have more peace than I have ever felt before.

Wife 2

My husband and I have been married over seven years. I have been disrespectful and controlling the entire time. About a month leading up to the day that I apologized, my husband had completely withdrawn from me. He barely talked to me, wouldn't look at me, and tried to avoid me as much as possible. He started standing up to me (he had been very passive before), and there was really no physical intimacy. He also stated that he was done with our relationship; however he wasn't going to seek a divorce. He talked about moving out. It was during this time that I started crying out to God for my marriage. . . . I finally was convicted that my actions toward my husband were sin. I had known I was controlling all along, and I knew it wasn't good, but I don't know that I thought it was sin. My husband has sinned greatly against me, with more "obvious" sins, so it was easier to justify the "little" sin of control.

I knew I needed to apologize and one night he told me that I didn't respect him, that I didn't accept who he was . . . that I always put our daughter and my family first, and that he didn't think I had forgiven him for things he had done. Normally, I would have tried to fight and defend myself, but I knew what I had to do. I agreed with him that I had done all those things. I said, "You're right. I'm sorry that I did all those things to you. I hurt you. The Lord has convicted me of what I've done and I want to change." He was very, very angry. He didn't believe me. He had no reason to and I knew that I couldn't expect him to believe that I was sincere. We had had talks like this before and while I was sorry he felt that way and I wanted to change, I failed each time. In his anger, he said, "You don't get to try anymore." He also told me that what I was doing was trying to manipulate him and he said, "You'll never change" and "You're only trying because we're on the rocks." I let him say all those things without defending myself, because I knew from there that my actions had to show him I was serious.

It's been almost three months since I fully submitted to the Lord in this area and since I apologized. He has definitely been very skeptical and tried to push me to see if I was sincere. I don't expect that trust to come quickly. It took almost eight years to get this far along, so it could take a long time to come out of it. At one point, he told me, "You're just stuffing it all inside." He believed I was just making an outward change but not an inward change to try to get him to stay. During this time, we had some peaceful periods and I thought things were getting better. Then I would mess up and he would jump to the extreme of wanting to leave me and saying that we will never work out or that he doesn't want us to work out. I haven't been perfect, of course, but I'm different than I was in the past. I apologize quickly now if I find myself disrespecting him. He's very sensitive to ways that I try to control him and he lashed out in anger (verbally) a few times when I tried to exert control over him.

Overall, I can't believe the changes in our marriage in just three months. I still have some fear that one day he'll just leave me, but I am just trying to trust in God that He's working in this situation and He's free to work on not only me, but also my husband as He sees fit, since I'm no longer standing in the way. Mainly in the last month, I've seen some really positive changes as my husband has started being physically affectionate with me again and joking and playing around with me. He seems to want to spend time with me and he started talking about the future. He started telling me some of his desires (in the past, I always shot down his ideas and desires if they weren't something I liked), and he's been more involved at home.

Wife 3

When I apologized to my husband he got angry and said my disrespect was partly his fault. He said he should've been harder on me. . . . He said he'd like to be happy about this and recognized my courage . . . but that he just wasn't ready for all that. He was skeptical. That was five months ago. I followed it right up with homework for myself to keep moving forward and focused on *The Respect Dare* by Nina Roesner.[1] Such a blessing! It kept me going through the times he baited me to test me. I also read several books from your list of your favorite marriage books [see appendix] and worked on things like boundaries. Now he's beginning to change and I find myself being skeptical. We have not had the major bouts of anger that overwhelmed our marriage last year. I'm learning so much patience. God has been very good to me! My biblical submission has definitely saved my marriage and softened a critical, dominant husband.

Wife 4

I did not apologize in the very beginning. I wanted to see how this respect thing would really play out. I started being more respectful to him and saw major changes in the way he behaved, including—but not limited to—being more loving to me! What a blessing to be able to personally watch our God work in my husband's heart. I have also started reading *Love and Respect* by Dr. Emerson Eggerichs and one night my husband asked me about the book. Well, that night I had him *so* intrigued with this whole concept. We had a great long talk (my hubby is not usually the long talk kind of guy), and I "officially" apologized then. His reaction was kind of like, "Wow! Who the heck am I talking to? Are you really my wife?" I felt so connected to him that night and I know he felt close to me, too. I feel overall that my hubby is skeptical, but with God's gracious guidance, I will press on and have faith that my husband will see that the new me isn't going anywhere.

Wife 5

I didn't apologize until I was several months along in my new respectful, peaceful life. When I first felt convicted by God to change my ways, my husband and I had been married for 20 years . . . and I had never heard of the *Love and Respect* concept of marriage. I came from a broken home and was never exposed to a godly marriage. I had no idea how to relate to my husband. I was fearful and controlling. . . . I began by deciding to trust my husband and respond enthusiastically to his sexual needs. Just doing those things made such a positive difference in our relationship! It wasn't until 2008 that I put a name to my and God's "marriage repair plan" when I heard (about) a new book called *For Women Only* by Shaunti Feldhahn.[2] Eye opening! . . . At first I was just trying to improve my marriage, but after reading Feldhahn's book, God began convicting me of *my* sin. . . . My apology came spur of the moment one day when we were cuddling and I said, "I wish so much that I could go back and do our earlier marriage years over. I treated you badly without even meaning to." He was aghast. "How?" he asked. I replied, "I was disrespectful to you and your leadership in our family." He grinned and hugged me saying, "That's alright!" (He is not a long talk kind of man.) Today is our 31st wedding anniversary and we are doing very, very well! I know that we would never have made it to this milestone without God opening my eyes to my sin. Every husband is different but I think mine would not have responded favorably to an apology at the beginning. He would have seen it as an empty ploy to manipulate him more. For me, waiting until he had already seen permanent changes in my attitude was key.

Ladies, I hope that these wives' stories might encourage and inspire you to seek God's wisdom for you about what steps God might want you to take to make things right in your marriage, if there is a need to do so. My prayer is that you might be sensitive to God's voice and leadership rather than rushing into something. Sometimes we will wait a long time until He shows us that the time is right. Sometimes, He shows us we need to act immediately. God is able to give you the words, the wisdom, the timing, and the approach that will be best for your husband if you need to repent to him for something. You might just be surprised how liberating apologizing and true humility can be.

My Husband Shares His Heart

G reg has played a huge role in my journey to become a godly wife. Interestingly, he used to really hate it when I read marriage books earlier in our marriage. He felt like he was my "guinea pig," and that I was experimenting on him—trying to change him and "fix" him. But after I read *Love and Respect* by Dr. Eggerichs, Greg began doing some research to help me find similar books because he saw that I wanted to learn and understand all I could about respect and becoming a godly wife. Over time, he became willing to have long discussions with me about the things I read. Sometimes I ask questions and write down his answers because I want to remember everything he says. I'm thankful that Greg has allowed me to share his thoughts with you. I pray that his words might give you some interesting ideas to ponder. Perhaps his words might be a catalyst for some deep, healing discussions in your marriage one day, as well.

GREG'S REFLECTIONS ON MY JOURNEY
FROM 2008 TO 2011

Greg: I have a secret, one that you might find hard to believe. I never asked April to do any of the stuff she advocates so strongly. In fact, I probably was a little annoyed at times when she would want to do some of these things. In retrospect, most of the time it was my own ignorance that would bother me. I know I had the same questions that some of you may have.

- What would other people think?
- Won't they think I'm an abusive husband or something?
- Nobody does that anymore!
- That's "old school thinking" that doesn't apply today.
- Is she going to embarrass me?
- Aren't people going to think she is a little "different"?

She began to ask me questions multiple times a day such as, "When I did this, did you feel respected?" or "Was I disrespectful when I did this or said this?" Most of the time, I was not totally sure if I felt respected or disrespected. I hadn't really thought about whether something was the right or wrong way to approach an issue in a long time. I noticed a lot of changes beginning to take place. April asked me to start keeping track of the finances—something I didn't mind doing—but it was something she had taken care of since we got married. I also noticed that she started telling me things that she was interested in doing and then she let them be. She fully relied on my decision on these interests, and if I didn't immediately give her a decision, I didn't hear about them again. I didn't have to put up any fences to give myself time to think on things for once. I didn't feel rushed. I didn't always get to even have input on a lot of decisions before. Sometimes her attitude was, "This is the way it is going to be, do you understand?" Other times she had consumed herself with a decision all day and when I didn't immediately have the answer she was looking for, it just wasn't worth it to me to argue about it with her.

April had been a pretty tough standard for me to measure up to. I often felt diminutive next to her in her decision making and very much so in spiritual things. She painted every decision so definitively in black and white that I thought I must be a little "off" to see any gray areas, even if I thought we needed to allow a little grace for this or that. But all of a sudden, during this time frame she began making sure I made family decisions. At this point, I didn't know what was going on. All of a sudden, I had an ever-increasing load on my shoulders that I never had before. It was as if April was unloading all of the weight that she had carried for so many years. She put some of the weight under my care, but most of it really didn't need to be carried around in the first place. April seemed happier than she had been in years. She had some spark that I hadn't seen since we were first married. She was better able to concentrate on what the kids needed and she kept the house better than it had been before. She seemed to get what I really was thinking now.

I was a little alarmed by all of these changes. I hate change. I was still a bit skeptical about whether this was a fad or just a momentary upswing that would not last. Strangely, I had a large amount of decision making added to my plate and, yet, it felt kind of neat. I felt an unbelievable sense of responsibility to take all of my family's interests to heart to make every decision. It wasn't that I didn't do that before, but knowing that my wife had put her complete trust in my decision, I was compelled to make sure that the decision was best for all of us. I really have come to the point in making decisions that I do not even consider my own interests anymore.

One huge change occurred at this time. On the days when April was not working late as a pharmacist, it didn't matter what she was doing when I came home, she would stop everything and come give me the biggest hug and tell me how much she missed me. She would have dinner well under control and then she would give me a few minutes to unwind before supper was ready. She intentionally gave me a few minutes to make the conversion from work to home. The kids seemed happier to see me come home from work and also welcomed me with a great big, "Welcome home, Daddy!" when I came in.

It was as if she had had spiritual "eye surgery" so that her vision changed to only see my best, to only appreciate my gifts, and to be blinded to any false expectations or negative feelings about me. Another change I saw was in April's spirit. She often had her quiet times just about every morning, but the tone of her Bible study and prayer time changed. I often felt before like she took all of my negative traits to God and asked Him to change me. During this time, though, it was different. It was like she had accepted me in her prayer time. She thanked God each day for all of my strengths and asked God to use those strengths in a powerful way. She also put her trust in God that He was in control of her life and our marriage. She decided that letting God have control allowed her to trust in my ability to lead our marriage.

So, you are thinking that April basically cut off her feelings and emotions, right? Fortunately, her changes only opened up our communication to levels we had never seen. Now that we didn't have to battle with the negative barriers, we could talk openly and in a way that I could safely be close enough to her to understand her feelings. When my negative baggage disappeared from our relationship, it helped me look beyond my wife's faults as well. I will be honest: she wasn't perfect. She had times when she stumbled occasionally, but she would get right back up and work even harder to correct her mind-set. It was a learning process for her and she continues to learn. I can also tell you that I wasn't always the perfect test subject either. I probably was not as consistent as I needed to be in stepping up to lead in our marriage. It still is a learning process for me, as well. Before my wife started trying to become a godly wife, I loved her and that did not change. After April became a more godly wife, we have been able to have an effective marriage that makes each of us thrive. I fell in love with April because she was a go-getter, ready to tackle anything, extremely capable, intelligent, beautiful, a believer in Christ, and an extraordinary woman. Some of those qualities contributed to issues we were having in our marriage. After April became respectful and biblically submissive, she is still all of those things, but I would describe her as empowered to enjoy and prosper our marriage. Her example has encouraged me to try to be a better husband, to try to learn her language better, and to learn to help her work through her feelings.

My Interview with Greg in 2013

I asked Greg what his perspective was earlier in our marriage as I was unknowingly being so disrespectful and controlling. During that time, he became very quiet, passive, and unplugged. There were times he barely spoke to me, barely looked at me, and sometimes barely touched me. This interview is the first time I had ever heard many of these particular thoughts of Greg's. I thank and praise God every day for the miracles He did in our marriage. It is all Him. I pray this conversation might enrich your marriage.

April: What are some of the things I did that used to bother you the most before God showed me my disrespect and control?

Greg: You had this conversation in your head with me all day long and were already mad at me before I could even say what I wanted to say. You already decided what my answer was going to be and how you were going to deal with it—there was no use in me answering.

You would ask me a question, but it was worded so that if I picked one answer, I would have to be the stupidest person in the world. There was only one right answer. I couldn't disagree with you. That was not allowed. You knew you were "so right" about it, there was no room for you to be wrong. There was no room for any other perspective.... Once you are hit with that over and over, why answer? What's my role? Do I have a role?

April: How did you feel when I wanted to talk and "connect" with you forty hours per week or more?

Greg: I don't even talk to myself forty hours per week! To me as a man, talking equals conflict. At work, we have to have a meeting because there is a problem. At home, we have to talk because there is a problem. It was never, "Can we talk about what you want to talk about, honey?" It was always, "I'm going to tell you, and you're going to listen to me."

April: Why did you stay with me all those fourteen-plus years that I was not giving you what you needed?

Greg: There were times I wasn't happy. I stayed because I loved you. Leaving wasn't an option. I could be unhappy, but it didn't mean I didn't want you to be my wife.

April: Were there any happy times for you?

Greg: There were some happy times. My perspective was, if I didn't want some of your characteristics, I shouldn't have married you. Some of the things that made you struggle a little bit at being a wife were some of the things that attracted me to you as well. I liked that you were intelligent, a go-getter, and had a little bit of an edge of brazenness. I liked that you were independent, strong-willed, and educated. I didn't want to be with somebody that was "just average." You wouldn't do anything that you didn't give it 110 percent. School, flute, piano, pharmacy—you gave everything you had to all of it. You were also good with words. I thought it would help me somewhere in the long run.

April: What were some of the hardest things for you during those years?

Greg: I felt like I didn't have a voice. I wasn't not answering you to try to irritate you at all. I felt trapped in my situation. It didn't matter if I answered. It seemed like however I saw things, it wouldn't matter.

April: There were a handful of times that you really stood your ground, and I ended up *very* reluctantly doing what you wanted. Why were you willing to insist on those few issues?

Greg: If I lost those types of things, I wouldn't have had anything to call my own. I wasn't willing to lose those things.

April: How did the way I disrespected and controlled you impact your relationship with God?

Greg: I don't know that you had a real negative effect on my relationship with God. But your "mastering" of it would come into play. When it came to Bible knowledge, you were way, way, way beyond where I was.

When it came to wisdom, . . . we all had issues . . . due to a lack of experience and maturity. I don't think you had a huge role in disparaging me spiritually.

April: Did you have any hope that I would change?

Greg: I was not looking for you to change. I knew there were ways we could be better. I looked at myself as the problem most of the time. I looked at me as "not getting it." I didn't look at you as the problem. I just wasn't doing what I needed to do. I wasn't making you as happy as I needed to. I was not the husband I needed to be. I was looking for ways to limit the pain by going into a shell.

April: I believe that if you had told me I had hurt you at any point in those first fourteen-plus years, I would have felt horrible and would have wanted to apologize and make things right. But you never said a word. Never. I eventually believed you didn't have feelings at all. Why did you suffer silently all those years?

Greg: I didn't tell you my pain because "a man doesn't show pain."

April: Why did you allow me to lead?

Greg: With some issues I figured it was advantageous for you to lead. When I wouldn't make a decision, you were always there to hammer down the decision, and if things got screwed up, it was your fault.

April: I can remember begging you many times, "Please, just tell me what you need! I don't know what you need!" Why didn't you say that you needed respect from me? Why didn't you say you needed me to stop trying to control you?

Greg: 1) I felt like it was my problem. 2) I didn't necessarily know what I needed. 3) I felt like it would have been selfish for me to say what I needed.

I knew I needed respect, but I didn't know how to explain that to you. I didn't look at it as something I could ask for. I looked at is as something I couldn't obtain. There was something I was doing that meant I didn't deserve it.

April: When I began to honor and respect you, were you ever tempted to be hateful and mean to me?

Greg: No.

April: Did you think, "Great, now I can do anything I want and I don't have to consider her feelings at all?"

Greg: I don't think I changed very many things about the way I treated you. I opened up more because I didn't feel like the target. It didn't mean that I went and did things with abandon or recklessly. I didn't feel like a dog on a leash anymore because you weren't trying to control me. Afterward, we were still attached, but by something stronger than control—trust. Some of the things I wanted weren't as important once I felt respected. I didn't need to look to other things as much for fulfillment.

April: How long was it before you began to feel safe with me again?

Greg: It took about three and a half years into your journey for me to feel safe with you. It was a gradual thing. There were many stages:

1. When is the honeymoon going to be over and the disrespect, pride, and control going to come back?

2. I'm not sure about all these things; they are a little quirky and kind of weird.
3. It is kind of weird, but there are some positive aspects to it.
4. She really seems to be doing this for the long term.

April: How did you feel when I stepped down from leading and just stopped taking over?

Greg: Decisions were kind of forced on me. I don't know if it was bad or not; I didn't have much choice. Things seemed like they needed to be done, so I knew I needed to do them. These were building-block type of things to help me feel like I could make decisions.

April: When did you realize I was going to support your decisions?

Greg: We were going to Charlotte, and you were reading two books: *The Proper Care and Feeding of Husbands* and *The Surrendered Wife.*[1] That trip comes to mind; I realized you were serious and then I was willing to get you whatever book might help you further.

April: When I first submitted to you, I was terrified that you would ask me to work more hours as a pharmacist and not be home with our children as much. Why didn't you insist that I work more?

Greg: I knew you wouldn't be happy if I told you that you had to work more.

April: At the time, I believed you saw no value in me being at home and being with the kids and only valued me if I was making money.

Greg: I valued all of those things, but I also valued paying bills and the ability to enjoy some luxuries in life and eating out occasionally.

April: Why did you not tell me you valued me being home, too?

Greg: In my mind it was because you were so adamantly screaming that you wanted to be home so badly. Affirming that didn't seem to be

the best thing to do. I didn't like the idea of having no air conditioning in the summer or heat in the winter. When your hours were cut at
work [December 22, 2009], that was a very traumatic time for me. We
had to take the kids' Christmas and birthday presents back two days
before Christmas. For me, gifts are a real big thing. You had been working more. Things were starting to be great. Our finances were in good
shape. We bought some new furniture. Then all that crashed down.
Taking things back to the store was embarrassing to me. Then when
you decided to be thankful that you could be home more, I thought,
"I am not okay. I am the worst provider and the worst husband. I am
depressed and embarrassed. April thinks it's a blessing that she is not
working and it's everything she wanted and she's happy." All my positive thoughts and plans went kaput. It shook my faith. You were praying for us not to be materialistic. I felt you were praying for God to be
against us.

More of Greg's Thoughts:

A husband wants to do everything he can for his wife. He wants
her to be happy. When she honors him, it makes him more sensitive to
what she wants and to her feelings. Every time he feels disrespected it is
like the clock setting back; every time he feels respected the clock goes
forward, motivating him in the marriage.

WHAT WE CAN LEARN

I think it is significant that both of us thought that Greg was the
whole problem. Yikes! The truth is, we were both contributing to the
problems in our marriage, and change only happened for me after I
was willing to look at my part in the mess. My power came when God
opened my eyes to my own sin and I began to focus on my life and
my relationship with Christ. Thankfully, when a woman biblically submits to and respects her husband, she has the freedom to speak her
mind and voice her feelings. Her husband, as he feels more and more

respected and honored, will generally desire what is in her best interest. A believing man who is entrusted with leadership reacts with humility, sacrificial love, and a desire to delight his wife. But more than that, his first priority is to please and honor Christ. Even an unbelieving husband, who is a fairly decent man, will eventually generally respond with humility and love to his wife's obedience to God's commands for her as a wife. Of course, this can take time, and there are no guarantees. Some husbands don't ever change. But if our husbands *are* going to become more loving, selfless, and godly, our path to get to that place is for us to begin to obey God first.

> "The truth is, we were both contributing to the problems in our marriage, and change only happened for me after I was willing to look at my part in the mess."

Greg was totally capable of leading. He does a wonderful job of it now! It took time for him to slowly begin to lead and to grow in leadership after me taking charge for so long. Before, I was sabotaging him, our marriage, and myself and didn't even know it. I never, ever, ever want to go back to the way things were. I was miserable, lonely, anxious, stressed, and fearful many times. Greg was shut down, depressed, passive, and emotionally very distant. Our marriage began to slowly heal when God showed me His design for marriage. Now, we have the intimacy and connection we both always wanted. My husband is the man I always knew he could be. I am the woman I had always longed to be. Not perfect, of course, but through the Holy Spirit's power, we are both light-years beyond where we were for so long. This is a lifelong journey of learning for us all. I am excited when I think about all of the growth, learning, maturing, and refining that God has in store for me.

Learning the Language of Respect

We have largely forgotten about the lost art of respect in our culture today. Genuine respect is something that everyone in our lives would appreciate, but especially our husbands. Some things are respectful to all men across the board. Some things are more unique to specific individuals. My purpose is to get you in the ballpark of respect and give you some ideas of places to start. It will be up to you to figure out and study what is respectful to your particular husband. Please don't try to implement all of my suggestions at once! That is totally unrealistic. This is a long, slow process. Pick out a few things to start with. Then maybe you can add one or two a week or so, as God leads you to. Take this in little baby steps and little bites at a time.

It is possible for a wife to turn my suggestions in this book into a score sheet and make it into something very legalistic. That is not my goal or intention at all. More important than my suggestions will be what your husband needs and what God's Spirit leads you to do in particular situations. God is the key here, not a list. It may be that some things that are really important to your husband aren't even covered in this book. Also, please remember that perfection is not the goal here. None of us will ever be totally perfect. The goal is to learn to speak this new masculine language more and more fluently and to bless your husband as you honor and obey God. It may take many months, maybe years, to really feel like you know how to speak this language well.

God's intention is for us all to witness godly marriages and thousands of beautiful examples of parents showing godly love and respect for each other as children grow up. His intention is for us to have godly examples in the church and community around us so that we would know how to speak love and respect to our husbands when we got married. Unfortunately, our culture, even in the church, has veered so far away from God's design for marriage, masculinity, and femininity that there are very few godly examples for the younger generations to follow today. In fact, disrespect for people in general, but especially for men, is normal and mainstream. So, respect will feel foreign and awkward at first because we aren't used to seeing or hearing it and we aren't used to thinking, speaking, and acting like this. We aren't even used to seeing other women treat men with respect. This language will begin to feel more natural and normal in time as we practice it and as we seek God with all our hearts. God will transform our minds and give us new hearts as we seek Him above all else. We can't do it on our own. Thankfully, this can be done with God's help!

WHERE TO START

So how do you get started? Some wives might share a list of ideas with their husbands of things that could be respectful and ask their men to check which suggestions might be meaningful to them. Some wives simply ask their husbands something like, "I would love for you to think about and share with me the three most disrespectful things I sometimes do, and the three things that would most speak respect to you. There is no rush; I would just really appreciate your insights." Some husbands are happy to give their input. Some husbands aren't able to verbalize what they would like or aren't willing to have conversations about these things until much later. If your husband is not able to share what would feel respectful to him, I believe you will find inspiration here.

For a lot of husbands who are feeling very disrespected or wounded and have shut down, a wife's words mean nothing to them at this point. In such cases, I suggest that you pray for God to show you which ideas to try first. Just begin trying a few new potentially respectful things and see how it goes. Pray that God will direct you to those things that will actually be affirming to your husband. If he likes going fishing in order to spend time alone, then going fishing with him will likely not improve your relationship! Just keep seeking God and trying to learn all He has for you to learn to be the woman He desires you to be. If you realize that your husband doesn't like a certain thing, write that down to keep in mind and listen to his feedback with interest. When you fall, repent, ask God to fill you with His power to walk in obedience to Him, and get right back up!

> "Do respectful things just to bless your husband, not to try to get him to change or to get something from him."

Your husband may not understand what on earth is going on when you start to change things. Some husbands may assume at first that change means manipulation. That is why it is good to take things slowly. I believe it is wise to stop all the intentional disrespect as soon as possible. Then, allow God and your husband to speak to you about unintentional disrespect. Slowly add some truly respectful things. Your husband may not believe you at first when you begin to honor and respect him. He may think you are mocking him or being sarcastic when you say you trust him or when you don't get upset when he makes a mistake. If he gets upset when you genuinely try to show him respect, please be patient. It is going to take time (many months or years) for him to accept that your respect is for real. Don't give up or get discouraged. Just gently reiterate, "Sweetheart, I really *do* trust you now. I know you aren't used to that, but I am serious about this." (Be sure that you do trust him if you are going to say that to him!) Do respectful things just to bless your husband, not to try to get him to change or to get something from him. That would be manipulation. It can be helpful to think about dropping your expectations and just focusing on a desire to sincerely bless your husband and please God.

> *Lord,*
> *I desire to learn the language of masculine respect. Please erase any confusion in my mind. Help me not feel overwhelmed. Help me begin to understand my husband's perspective accurately. Help me to realize the feminine power You give me as a wife to build up, encourage, and honor my husband. I don't control or change my husband, but I trust that You may use me and my obedience to Your Word to inspire him as You accomplish Your good purposes in his heart.*
> *In the name and power of Christ, amen!*

WAYS TO RESPECT YOUR HUSBAND

There are many ways to show respect to your husband. Throughout the rest of this chapter I offer numerous ideas to help us learn and practice the language of respect. In addition to the ideas noted below, as God impresses additional ideas on your heart—ideas that relate specifically to your marriage—feel free to jot them in the margins, or keep a separate journal for this new journey! If your husband is willing to look at this chapter, or if you want to share some ideas with him, it would be amazing to get his input so that you can focus only on the things that really matter to him.

With Your Words

Scripture has much to say about how we as believers in Christ are to speak because our words reveal what is happening in our souls. They expose our true motives, priorities, goals, and plans. They expose hidden sin. Our words reveal our true level of spiritual maturity and devotion to Christ. Our words can be a source of great blessing, encouragement, strength, and joy when we use them in accordance with God's will. How does God desire for us to use words?

> Those who consider themselves religious and yet do not keep a tight rein on their tongues deceive themselves, and their religion is worthless. (James 1:26)

> The tongue has the power of life and death, and those who love it will eat its fruit. (Prov. 18:21)

> A gentle answer turns away wrath, but a harsh word stirs up anger. The tongue of the wise adorns knowledge, but the mouth of the fool gushes folly. (Prov. 15:1–2)

> Do not let any unwholesome talk come out of your mouths, but only what is helpful for building others up according to their needs, that it may benefit those who listen. (Eph. 4:29)

Here are some ideas for respecting your husband with your words:

- Speak highly of your husband to others in the family, to your children, to your coworkers, to your friends, to God, and to yourself! Focus on Philippians 4:8 things about your husband: things that are true, noble, right, pure, lovely, admirable, excellent, or praiseworthy.
- Check with your husband before sharing a confessional story involving him with a Bible study group, family members, or friends.

He wants to know he won't be embarrassed by something you might share.

- Until you know how to speak respectfully, just focus on not being disrespectful. Silence generally comes first in this process. In time, you can build your level of speaking as God shows you how to do that in ways that are life-giving to your husband.
- Ask for things with a friendly, pleasant tone of voice, and a smile whenever appropriate. Give your husband time to think without pressuring him.
- Be gracious about accepting "no" or "wait." Do not try to force him to see or do things your way.
- Praise your husband to your children, both when he is present and when he is away.
- Compliment his intelligence, talents, gifts, and abilities—a sentence or two a few times per week, for example.
- If your husband doesn't like compliments, show him respect in ways that are meaningful to him personally, without words.
- Give suggestions or share requests humbly instead of giving commands or directives. "I would love it if..." "Would you please help me with ...?" "I would really appreciate ..." "Sometime tonight, I would like to ..."
- If you have concerns or questions, learn to ask for clarification in a non-threatening, friendly, supportive way. Maybe try words like, "Would you please tell me more about ..." or "Would you please clarify this for me?" or "I want to be sure I understand—is this what you have in mind ...?" instead of "Why would you ...?" or "Why did you ...?"
- If your husband sins against you, take care of any sin in your own life first and spend time in prayer before approaching him about it very humbly and gently (Matt. 7:1–5; 18:15–17).
- Do not threaten divorce or use the word *divorce* about your marriage.

- Filter every word that comes out of your mouth through respect for God and for your husband.

For me, controlling my words is the most difficult spiritual challenge I face (other than controlling my thoughts). James 3 is completely devoted to "the tongue." James says, "We all stumble in many ways. Anyone who is never at fault in what they say is perfect, able to keep their whole body in check" (3:2). God is very interested in how we use our words and our mouths. In fact, if God's Spirit is in control of our mouths, the rest of godliness will be "easy" in comparison. Reflect a bit on how you use your words with your husband. This might be a good exercise to do during your daily Bible reading and prayer time.

> *Lord,*
> *Please help me to examine how I have been using my words. Am I pleasing You with the way I speak to my husband? Is there anything that needs to change about the specific words I choose to use, my motives, or the content of my messages to my husband? Is there anything unwholesome or destructive in my words? Please give me insight and clarity on the things I'm doing well and the things I need to change so that I might better honor You and my husband.*
> *In the name of Christ, amen.*

Through Nonverbal Communication

This one is even more difficult than controlling our words, in my view, and it is connected very closely with my thought life. If I have my words totally under control and what I say is respectful and a blessing, but my tone of voice, body language, facial expressions, and eyes are sending a message that is disrespectful or hateful, I have a big problem. I have never been good at lying or faking anything. My tone of voice and nonverbal signals have always given my real intentions and meaning away to anyone. It is important for us to allow God's Spirit to have so much control that, in time, we are no longer even thinking the disrespectful, contentious, hateful thoughts, generally speaking. Jesus said it this way:

> "The eye is the lamp of the body. If your eyes are healthy, your whole body will be full of light. But if your eyes are unhealthy, your whole body will be full of darkness. If then the light within you is darkness, how great is that darkness!" (Matt. 6:22–23)

Our eyes reveal the intentions and motives of our hearts. Our countenance and our facial expressions communicate a wealth of information about the sincerity of our respectful words. Our nonverbal language confirms and strengthens our respectful words and gives them great weight. At first, when we are learning respect, just stopping the disrespectful words is about all we can do. But in time, we begin to mature and grow. We move from holding back disrespect, to speaking respectfully, and then to allowing God's Spirit to give us control over our nonverbal body language and tone of voice.

Some husbands may be receptive to affection, and that is a wonderful way to express respect without words. Your friendly, affectionate touch—a hand on his shoulder, high-fiving him as you walk past in the hallway, a hug now and then, a hand on his thigh when you sit beside him—can show him that you care about him, are connecting with him, and that you adore him. If he is not receptive, he may be more receptive to your touch in the future as he heals, or this may be part of his personality. That will require God's discernment and wisdom for each wife to decide how to bless and honor her husband with touch. Some husbands may feel smothered by touch; others may love affectionate touching often.

As a Grown Adult and Equal

I can show Greg real respect by acknowledging his right to his own opinions, desires, feelings, ideas, and choices just like I have a right to these things for myself. He is not my little boy and I am not his mother. The reverse is also true: I am not Greg's little girl and he is not my father. There is not a parent/child dynamic in God's design for marriage. So, I can release Greg from my expectations that he be another me—or that he be a woman—and give him room to be himself and to be masculine in his own unique way. I can accept him as he is without making him my "project," as if he is in dire need of my wisdom and help to "fix" him. I can make sure to ask him for his ideas and opinions and show him that I care very much about what he thinks. I can give the same weight to Greg's way of doing things that I give to my way. These are things I would certainly do for a dear girl-friend. I can show my faith and respect for Greg by acknowledging that we are on equal ground before God and we are fellow travelers, rather than thinking of myself as being better than Greg or thinking that he is better than me. This is how I would want Greg to treat me, as well.

Here are some ideas to show your husband you see him as his own person and an adult:

- Assume he can handle his relationships with his boss, his parents, his siblings, and his friends without your help. If he feels he needs help, he will ask for help.
- Realize that your husband is just as loved by God, just as important in your family, and just as much an image bearer of God as you are.
- Allow him to make his own decisions about how to spend his time. Give him freedom to be with his friends, work on a hobby, enjoy a football game, and do what he wants to do without making him feel guilty or getting upset. You can ask for what you

would like him to do with you in a friendly way, without pressure. "I'd really love to spend some time together this week."
• Wait for him to ask you for help before you jump in.

I had to modify the Golden Rule ("Do to others as you would have them do to you."—Luke 6:31) a bit in my mind as a wife. Instead of trying to show love to Greg the way I would want him to show it to me, I seek to meet and honor his unique and masculine needs the way I would want him to seek to meet and honor my feminine and individual needs. I am willing to give him what he desires and needs rather than trying to give him what I desire and need.

As the Most Important Man in the World to You
When Greg and I got married, God joined us together as one in His sight. I have a relationship and covenant with Greg that I don't have with any other person on the planet. I want to be sure that I treat Greg with more honor, kindness, gentleness, love, blessing, and goodness than I give to anyone else. I have the privilege and responsibility of ministering to this one man using the most powerful expressions of femininity God has created. My husband is my most important human ministry, followed by our children. If I want to do something for God's kingdom, it has to start in my marriage, in my view. How can I treat other people with greater attention, consideration, importance, or respect than I treat my own husband? He should get the absolute best I have to offer. Yes, he sees me at my worst sometimes, too. But how I long for him to experience my very best self as God transforms me.

"My husband is my most important human ministry, followed by our children."

I want to communicate to Greg that he is the most special and most respected man in my life. I want to do that by taking his opinions into consideration before anyone else's. I want to go to him first for advice. I want to call him first when there is a big problem or when there is something wonderful to share. I want to treat him like he is truly the most important person in the world when we see each other after work each day. If he asks me to help him, I want to try to do whatever I can to make his concerns my priority. Maybe I could seat him at the place of honor at the dinner table or serve him before the children as some wives do. I might let him lead the way at the store or if we are driving separate cars. I could let him handle things that he knows a lot more about than I do, showing him my trust in his abilities to take care of things. I want to give him all of my very brightest, most trusting smiles, my best manners, my undivided attention whenever possible, my greatest love (in a human relationship), and I want to be sure he knows that I care about what is important to him. I do need to be careful not to make Greg more important than Christ to me; that is always a subtle temptation we must guard against. But in all of my human relationships, there should be an obvious distinction in the way I treat my husband that shows to anyone who observes me that my husband has first place in my life under God.

In Your Own Relationships

Respect goes much further than just something you do for your husband. As believers in Christ, God also calls us to respect Him first, to respect others, and to respect ourselves. Respect is part of love. If I love someone, I don't want to be rude, condescending, or oblivious to that person's needs. I will treat others with thoughtfulness, consideration, and care. Even though disrespect is rampant in our culture, my life can be an oasis of respect that flows in every direction, bringing healing, love, and joy to everyone I touch.

1. By Reverencing and Obeying Christ

There are many ways I can show respect and reverence for Jesus. The more I get to know Him and His character, the more I can exhibit respect, because the more I know about His holiness and perfection, the more I understand how worthy He is of my respect. The more I read His Word and take what He says seriously and seek to obey His Word, the more respect I am showing for Him. You may enjoy studying about the character and attributes of God so that you can discover new things about which to respect and reverence Him. A great place to start might be to listen to "The Character of God" and "God's Providence" by Wayne Grudem in his podcasts of "Systematic Theology." Or you may want to listen to sermons by David Platt or John Piper about the character of God to fill your mind with knowledge of His goodness and things about which you can praise Him.

Some other ways you can show respect for Christ would be:

- Find your contentment, purpose, strength, identity, and acceptance totally in Christ no matter what your husband is or is not doing (Phil. 4:12–13).
- Have grace and mercy available to your husband just like God has for you (Matt. 18:21–35, parable of the unmerciful servant).
- Be a generous forgiver by God's power (Matt. 6:14–15).
- Be more concerned about obeying Christ, bringing glory to God, and seeking God's will than the outcome of an individual decision (Matt. 16:24).
- Trust God's sovereignty to cause even your husband's mistakes and sins to work out for your ultimate good and His ultimate glory (Rom. 8:28–30).
- Receive all that Jesus has done for you. Cherish and enjoy the abundant life He has prepared for you!
- Sing praises to God in your heart or out loud as you drive.
- Start a list of things for which you are thankful to God.

- Savor intimacy with Christ and stay in His Word and in fervent prayer daily. Let your thoughts and your heart dwell on Him throughout each day. Stay connected to the One who will never leave you or forsake you (John 15:1–8; Heb. 13:5).
- Invite the Holy Spirit into your life and allow Him to have full control. He will never be overwhelmed by any of your needs. He is able to flood your heart with His Living Water until you are overflowing with His love, joy, peace, patience, kindness, goodness, faithfulness, gentleness, and self-control (Gal. 5:22–23).
- Work out your own salvation with fear and trembling and seek to grow more in your faith and trust in Christ (Phil. 2:12–13).
- Count trials and problems as joy, because God will use them to strengthen and test your faith to bring you to greater maturity in Christ (James 1:2–4)!
- Remember that you represent Jesus to everyone you meet. You are His ambassador. Everything you say and do reflects on Christ to cause others either to think more highly of Jesus or to despise Jesus.

2. By Publically Supporting Your Husband

Respecting our husbands in private is a wonderful, marriage-building thing to do and it is critically important. But somehow, the way we relate to our husbands in front of other people carries even more weight with a lot of husbands. Our level of respect for them can dramatically impact the level of respect others have for them. When my husband's coworkers see that I deeply and genuinely respect my husband and treat him like a king, they may assume that he is more worthy of their respect, too. But if they see that I disrespect Greg, hold him in contempt, and treat him terribly, my disrespect can cause them to think something like, "That guy's wife knows him better than anyone, so her opinion of him is probably accurate." Then my husband's coworkers, boss, clients, church friends, neighbors, family members, and friends (especially men) may begin to lose respect for my husband. Or they may pity him that he has to put up with that kind of behavior from his wife, which may be even worse than other men losing respect for him. I am my husband's PR rep when I am around other people. What I do and say reflects on my husband in a profound way that greatly impacts his reputation and credibility with others. You may not have realized it before, but you represent your husband to other people. You are a reflection of his character in their eyes, and your husband is probably keenly aware of this fact.

> "I am my husband's PR rep when I am around other people. What I do and say reflects on my husband in a profound way that greatly impacts his reputation and credibility with others."

Here are some suggestions to show public support for your husband:

- Distance yourself from women who speak negatively and disrespectfully about their husbands.
- Don't let anyone speak poorly of your husband to you, if he is not there. (If he is there, he may prefer to defend himself rather than have you defend him.)
- Cultivate godly friendships with women who seek to honor God, to honor their husbands, and to honor your husband.
- Don't seek advice from women who don't treat their husbands well, or those who cherish any kind of sin in their hearts.
- If your husband doesn't like a particular group or friend of yours, gently ask about his concerns and then limit contact with the group or friend, if necessary. Many times, a husband's concern in a situation like this is another woman's disrespect for her own husband or for himself. If he feels these relationships are

detrimental to your spiritual life, your children, his leadership, or your marriage, seek to honor his preferences. Pray for him to have God's wisdom.*

- If your family undermines your husband, ask your husband how he would like you to handle the situation and do your best to co-operate with and honor your husband above your family. You have a covenant with him, not with them. You can treat your family with respect and honor, but be sure to treat your husband with the most respect and honor. If you must choose, your husband has to come first.

We've all seen the woman on Facebook who publically posts a three-thousand-word verbal assault against her man. It is not pretty. Unfortunately, even if a couple reconciles, there could be serious damage done to a man's reputation among extended family, friends, church members, and coworkers after a woman chooses this route. There are some men whose very careers could be threatened by a wife's angry tirade on social media. It can be almost impossible to undo that kind of damage in the minds of others. A woman who posts a malicious, disrespectful, hateful rant proves that she has evil motives, not godly love, for her husband. We destroy our chance as Christian women to shine for Christ to our online friends if we do this. When a Christian wife behaves like this in public, she maligns the gospel of Christ Jesus (Titus 2:5). How could this ever be worth the cost?

I would like to encourage us all to keep private relationship information private and off of social media. I don't believe it is ever appropriate to air our dirty marriage laundry in public. That is extremely disrespectful to our husbands and it destroys our witness for Christ. Our

---

*If a husband is extremely controlling and refuses to allow his wife to have any contact with anyone ever, that wife may need to prayerfully seek outside counsel, being careful to do so safely.

husbands need to be able to count on us not to attack them in front of others, even if they do something wrong or make a mistake at times. They need to know we are loyal and trustworthy. If you are having a lot of trouble in your marriage, you can go to a godly mentoring wife—an older, spiritually mature woman who lives out God's Word and is a prayer warrior—or a godly, Christian counselor. Other people do not need to know about the arguments, fights, or issues you are having with your husband.

In Ephesians 4:29–5:20, God's Word gives us a beautiful standard of how to use our words that we can apply to every area of our lives, even how we use social media. Take a minute to read these verses, then ask yourself, am I using God's standard in how I speak to others in person and on social media? Ask God to help you see areas that He wants to change.

Another way we can show honor and respect for our husbands and our marriages is by limiting the number of private messages, emails, phone calls, or texts between us and other men. Perhaps there are times when it would be appropriate to copy your husband on emails you send to other men. This is something I do and I think of it as a safeguard for myself, for Greg, and for the other man, as well.

3. By Respecting Yourself

Men tend to trust and care most about those they respect. If a wife treats herself with disdain and disrespect, she is unwittingly teaching her husband not to value or cherish her much either. Again, a man may think something like, "She knows herself better than I do. If she thinks she is worthless, maybe she knows something I don't." It is important for me not to think of myself as being better than Greg, but it is also important for me to properly value, cherish, love, and respect myself in healthy ways and to understand who I am and my worth in Christ. When a woman stands up firmly (and respectfully) for herself if she is being wronged, that says a lot to a man. It has been my experience that a husband tends to respect his wife to the degree that she respects herself in addition to the degree that she respects him.

A godly wife does not encourage her husband to treat her like garbage. If he is being hateful or hurtful, she has the right and responsibility to ask him to stop (Matt. 18:15). If he won't stop, she may decide to leave the room or the house for a time. She doesn't have to sin or be disrespectful to do this. She may decide to create some distance, if he does not stop or does not apologize in some way, until he does apologize. If he approaches her for sex or to ask her for something, she might softly but firmly say something like, "I wish I could do X with you, but I am still sad/angry/upset about what you said earlier." And that may be all she has to say, depending on how God's Spirit prompts her. Then he can decide if he wants to apologize for what he did that was wrong. (Please keep in mind that some husbands try to apologize without words by doing something kind. A wife may certainly decide to accept that kind of apology.)

Some suggestions for respecting yourself:

- Try to get enough sleep and take care of your own basic physical needs. If you are sleep-deprived, undernourished, sick, or exhausted, it is *really* hard to be a godly wife.
- Be comfortable in your own body. Enjoy the gift of your personal beauty. Don't compare yourself to the world's definition of beauty. Appreciate the beauty that God has given to you externally.
- Dress in a more feminine way. This often helps women cherish their own gift of femininity more. Each woman has her own fashion sense, preferences, and style. I am not suggesting we must all dress the same way, but it could be interesting to experiment to see if you feel more feminine when you dress in certain ways and to see if that impacts the way you and your husband relate. (This made a big difference for me personally in helping me to feel softer and more womanly.)

- Dress in a modest way in public to show respect for God, your body, your sexuality, your husband, and other men.
- Carry yourself well as much as possible. You are a precious daughter of the King of kings and Lord of lords if you belong to Christ, made in the image of God.
- Don't hate your body.
- Take care of your appearance. Don't make an idol out of thinness or beauty, but make some effort to take care of your physical body.
- Acknowledge when you are emotionally hurt. Softly say something like, "That hurts," or "That felt harsh. Please stop," if your husband says something abrasive. Be vulnerable and real without lashing out at him.
- If he sins against you, say something like, "This really wounds me. Please don't do that. It's not okay." Or maybe say, "When you do X, it hurts me very much." Of course, God may give you specific things to say in each situation.
- Acknowledge your limitations and that there are some things you just can't do.
- Allow yourself grace and mercy when you fall. You are human, too!
- Share your heart—and your full range of emotions, when appropriate—honestly, calmly, briefly (depending on your husband's personality), and sincerely with good manners. It is important to say that you feel sad, upset, nervous, scared, happy, thankful, peaceful, and so on. You can say these things, with sensitivity to God's Spirit and to your husband's needs.
- Seek to develop godly inner beauty that will last and grow over time.
- Savor the gift of godly femininity on every level: spiritually, emotionally, mentally, and physically. Enjoy being a woman of God! Study to learn what godly femininity means (see For Further Study at the back of this book). Embrace vulnerability and gentle-

ness. Be a soft, safe, welcoming sanctuary to your husband in this harsh world. Be willing to take shelter under his protection. Be a source of light and goodness by the power of God's Spirit working in you.

THE RESULTS OF LEARNING THE LANGUAGE

There are many, many ways in which we can show honor and respect to our husbands. A lot of these things actually require *less* time and effort than our old approach. I hope that a few of these ideas might inspire you to try a new way of relating to your husband. Not all of these suggestions will be your husband's cup of tea. But I have a feeling that some of them will meet some of his heart's masculine needs in powerful ways. In time, you may notice that there is a lot less tension in your relationship. You may realize you are both more relaxed and peaceful. And you will also probably discover that you both understand each other better and that you are able to communicate your needs and desires in a way that draws your husband to you instead of repelling him.

Instead of you and your husband arguing for hours or days, once he feels safe with you, all you may have to do is simply share your desire one time in a pleasant way and leave it with him. I just smile and ask for what I want in a friendly, pleasant tone of voice. A few months ago, I said, "Honey, I would really love for the kids to have a swing set." Then my husband started researching. He showed me ideas and I shared my thoughts. After a few weeks, he built an amazing swing set in the back yard and our children are enjoying it every day. If I need help with the trash now, I simply say, "Honey, would you please take out the trash when you get a chance? Thanks!" If I want to spend some time together, I might say, "Greg, I would love to go on a walk with you sometime tonight if you are up for it," or, "I'd love to spend some time cuddling with you tonight." (Now I know I am welcome to just sit beside him any time and cuddle if he is in bed or on the couch, so I don't really ask about that anymore.) If I need help with the kids, I might say, "Would you be able to put the kids to bed tonight, please? I need to take my pharmacy continuing education course online tonight at 8:00. Thanks so much!" Greg doesn't feel like he needs to resist me now because I am not competing with him or disrespecting him. He feels safe with me so he can hear my feelings, my heart, and my needs now in ways that he could not when there was so much tension between us.

We both get so much more of what we want now. I laugh when people tell me I must feel "oppressed." This is not oppression! It is the intimacy I always wanted but didn't know how to have. It took more than three and a half years to get to this place in our relationship. I don't miss our old ways at all. We are not perfect; we both still have a lot to learn, but God's ways are always very good, even if they don't make sense to us at first.

> "This is not oppression! It is the intimacy I always wanted but didn't know how to have."

Greg doesn't want that much from me at all. Sometimes this whole respect thing is surprisingly simple. Sadly, it took me a good six years into this journey to realize that Greg only desires a few things from me. I thought that the more I did, the better it would be for him. But it's really not that complicated. Greg likes for me to relax and cuddle with him in the evenings. He appreciates me taking care of the house and children (now he often helps me with particular chores). He doesn't want me to ask him what I can do for him. He doesn't need a lot of respectful words or actions from me. He likes for me to be happy and unstressed. Greg doesn't like a lot of change. He likes to make his own decisions about how he uses his time, but is happy to listen to my suggestions and concerns. Most of all, he just appreciates me being here with him and being his closest friend.

Greg told me that when I stopped all the criticism and negativity toward him, it was like someone removed the static from God's voice in his heart. Then, when I began to genuinely respect and follow him, he said it was like turning up the volume for the Holy Spirit. Wow! We have so much power as wives! We have the power to destroy our men or to inspire them to become all God desires them to be. How I pray we will use our power for good.

10

A Smorgasbord of Respect

L et's tackle some specific areas of our marriages and think through practical ways that we can show genuine honor and respect to our husbands. It would be wonderful if you grew up in a home where this kind of godly respect from your mom (as well as godly love from your dad) was your normal everyday experience. It would make it a lot easier for you to automatically know the respectful thing to do. Of course, your husband is not just like your dad, so even if your parents set a fantastic example, there will be some things that will need to be different in your marriage because you and your husband are a unique couple made up of unique individuals and personalities. Whether you had a great example or not, in Christ, you can learn to discard any ungodly examples you have seen and you can choose to learn to live in a godly way now. I think that is very good news!

> *Lord,*
> *Speak to me by the power of Your Spirit. Grant me Your wisdom, Your direction, and sensitivity to Your voice. Refine me. Make me a beautiful woman in Your sight. Cause me to become more and more like Christ and to shine brightly for You.*
> *In the name and power of Christ, amen!*

In Relation to His Prayers and Spirituality

My understanding is that the vast majority of Christian husbands, even pastors, do not pray with their wives. I love prayer and I believe in the power of prayer among God's people. I long to see all believing husbands pray with their wives, but we will need to be so careful here, ladies! This can be a very sensitive topic for a lot of husbands, not because they are not spiritual, necessarily, but because they may not want to be pressured, or they may feel that they are "putting on a show" if they pray in front of someone. Some people, both men and women, prefer not to pray out loud with others. That doesn't mean that they don't love God wholeheartedly or that they don't value prayer.

I think we can occasionally ask our husbands, "Would you please pray with me about this issue?" But I believe that some of us may find a lot of freedom and peace in just releasing this expectation altogether. If your husband can't or won't pray with you, please don't assume he doesn't love God or doesn't love you. Try just laying your hand on him at night and praying over him. Or pray for him during your time of private prayer. Ask God to empower him with wisdom to lead the family, to protect him from evil and temptation, and to fill him with the Holy Spirit. Trust God to work in him as you seek God's face in your own life with all your heart. The most important thing is that God is at work in your husband's life, which He is because He is sovereign and omnipotent.

I was surprised that I couldn't find one reference to any married couple praying together in Scripture. I also didn't find one direct command for husbands to pray with their wives. That was sobering to me. Maybe some of our expectations in this area are not even mentioned in the Bible at all. I personally had to apologize to my husband after I realized this because I had tried to pressure him to pray with me many times. In a survey I did on my blog, 66 percent of the husbands who responded said they prefer to pray privately. Most of the men who answered my survey also said that they pray without words at times. Let's give them grace and understanding to pray the way they want to pray as we seek God whole-heartedly ourselves. Joint prayer would be wonderful, in my mind, but Jesus values secret prayer greatly. We can always pray alone, knowing that our Father, who sees what we do in secret, will hear us (Matt. 6:6).

Here are suggestions for respecting your husband's spirituality:

- Don't criticize his frequency of praying or his actual prayers.
- Thank him for praying with you when he does.
- Don't interfere with his style of prayer.
- Tell him how much it means to you when he spiritually connects with you.
- Keep pursuing Christ privately yourself and seek to grow as deeply as you can in Jesus whether your husband seems to be growing or not. Don't feel like you have to wait for your husband to catch up. Your growth is dependent on Christ, not your husband.
- Don't correct his theology if it is just a minor issue or a matter of differing interpretation.
- Be content in Christ alone even if your husband doesn't pray with you. Prayer is primarily about you connecting with God, not your husband.
- Do be willing to question things that you believe are clearly major unbiblical doctrines or false teaching, first in your own heart and in your prayer time. Then seek God's wisdom about when and how to address the issue with your husband, or maybe start by asking clarifying questions: "Honey, I am confused. I read this passage and it seems to say this. What do you think?" God's Word may speak for itself in his heart. Or, if he is not a believer, God may prompt you to wait or not to attempt to bring this up (1 Peter 3:1–2).

Respecting Our Husbands When We Pray

Although I used to pray extensively for my husband earlier in our marriage, sadly, I had a disrespectful attitude toward my husband as I prayed, and I had an irreverent and disrespectful attitude toward God. I did not approach Him with proper fear and reverence. I didn't realize what I was doing at the time, but I approached God as if He needed to do what I told Him to do, and He needed to do it ASAP. God revealed to me a few years ago that if I want Him to hear my prayers, I must approach Him with reverence and a desire to obey Him in everything. He must be my greatest desire and highest priority. God also revealed to me that if I want Him to hear my prayers, I must approach Him with a genuine respect for my husband as well as for his God-given authority over me.

When I pray and seek God's will, I trust God to work through my husband and His plan for marriage. I don't say, "God, I'm going to totally ignore my husband that You gave me to lead me. I want You to lead me in the way I want You to, without me having to submit to Your design for marriage." God decides how to lead me and He decides the authority structure in marriage, the church, and the family, no matter what our culture says.

> "God decides how to lead me and He decides the authority structure in marriage, the church, and the family, no matter what our culture says."

One of the ways that I remind myself to approach God in humility and honor is to cover my head with a scarf or hat when I pray based on 1 Corinthians 11:3–16. This simple, tangible reminder helps me to adopt a respectful prayer posture in my soul—humbly approaching God and humbly acknowledging that God can and will lead me through Greg.

I am also careful to speak of my husband respectfully to God and not to bash Greg with spite or hatred in my heart. Whatever we say about our husbands, even in our own minds, becomes our perceived reality.

We can certainly share our concerns with God in a way that seeks to be constructive rather than a way that feeds resentment or bitterness.

Even if a husband is not a believer, God can and will lead a believing wife through him. She must be careful not to follow him into sin, but a wife in this situation can trust God's sovereignty to lead her through her husband just as much as a wife of a believing husband can trust God to lead her. God and our faith in God is the key, not our circumstances or our husbands.

As the Leader of Your Family

When it comes to their role as father, a number of husbands have shared with me that what they desire most from their wives are things like input and cooperation rather than criticism and opposition. I know I didn't realize the long-term consequences of my undermining Greg's authority with our children or on Greg's involvement with them. My husband had become very unplugged with our family. I was constantly asking him to do more with us and he seemed to ignore me. I thought he was just unloving. Now I know that I had disrespected him and taken over control. I wouldn't listen to him, wouldn't support his parenting, and thought I knew best since I had read more books about parenting. I wouldn't follow or cooperate with him, so he eventually gave up. It's incredibly heartbreaking to me to realize how destructive my attitude, words, and actions were at times. When a wife overrules or undermines a husband's decision, she unwittingly teaches their children to disrespect and ignore their father. By extension, she instructs her children to disrespect and ignore any person in authority.

Early in my journey into becoming a godly wife, I began to talk to our children (our son was seven and our daughter was two) and say things like:

- God made husbands/dads to be the leaders in the family.
- I was wrong to try to be in charge of things before. I am so sorry.

- We will all treat Daddy with respect, including me.
- Obey Daddy and Mama because God says for children to obey your parents so that you can have the best life (Eph. 6:1–3).
- If one of us says no to something, please don't ask the other parent. It will be no from both of us.
- Your Daddy asked you not to jump on the couch. I know he's not here right now, but we are going to honor him and obey him whether he is here or not.
- That decision is up to Dad (for bigger decisions). We will honor whatever he decides. You may ask for what you want respectfully, and you may explain why you would like to have what you want (usually one time, although there can be exceptions), and then accept whatever he decides is best.*

Children learn biblical submission to those in authority in their lives primarily from the way their mothers treat their fathers. I was shocked that when I began to change and treat Greg with much greater respect, our children immediately began to be so much more respectful to both of us. It scared me. I finally saw how closely they imitate the way I relate to Greg—my words, my tone of voice, my attitude—all of it. That is how they will treat any God-given authority. I am teaching them to either respect, honor, and submit to those in God-given authority in their lives or to disrespect and rebel against God-given authority now and in the future. Ultimately, I am teaching my children how to submit respectfully to Christ, as well—what a critical role! I have the honor of

---

*There can certainly be situations where it might be appropriate for a wife or child to respectfully appeal Dad's decision. This would require much prayer and a humble attitude. A wife or child might say, "Can we please talk about your decision about X? I have some additional information I believe may be critical to this decision. I believe this issue is extremely important because of Y. Would you please consider these concerns? Thank you." But then we can be calm and gracious whether the answer is yes or no. An appeal would be a rare thing, not standard operating procedure.

demonstrating respect and submission and living under the lordship of Christ to my precious children. This is my deepest desire as a mother, to train my children in godliness and to prepare them to love, honor, obey, and submit to Jesus as Lord.

Eventually, Greg started backing me up as a parent, too. Our children obeyed so much more readily! Their respect level for both of us went up even more when they saw us united as a team, honoring each other. My husband began to correct our children if they were disrespectful to me, too. My willingness to show respect and biblical submission to Greg has been one of the best things I have ever done as a parent! My change in attitude toward Greg has drastically impacted our children's attitudes, behavior, and obedience. My husband slowly began to stand taller, grow in his confidence as a husband, leader, and father, and plug back into the family. Now he is more and more the godly leader and loving dad and husband I always knew he could be.

The Church Decision

Many couples do not agree about where to go to church. The wife prefers one denomination or one worship style and the husband prefers another. Sometimes a wife just goes off on her own to the church she likes and refuses to go to church with her husband. I don't believe this is generally wise, unless the husband wants his wife to join him in a cult or false religion. A wife has the responsibility to share her feelings, opinions, ideas, and desires about what she would like in a church home (just as she should with any important decision). A husband needs a wife's perspective and valuable insight in order to collaborate to make the best possible decisions for the family. If a husband really doesn't have a preference or he sees that his wife has a strong desire to go to a certain church, he may decide to honor and support his wife's choice for a church home. If the husband and wife cannot agree, it is the husband's God-given responsibility to lead his family, taking his wife's feelings, concerns, and ideas into account. A wife in that situation can show respect and biblical submission by cooperating joyfully and willingly with her husband's decision even though she doesn't agree. She can use the "submitting under protest" concept (that we will discuss in chapter 11) if she feels very strongly against this decision. Or if she is not adamantly opposed to the church her husband prefers, she can say something like, "I really want to go to X church, and here are the reasons why. I don't want to go to Y church. Here are my reasons. Here are my feelings—I feel nervous about this. I am laying all of my concerns on the table, but I know that you will stand accountable to God one day for this decision, not me. So I will support whatever decision you believe is best and I trust you to lead us in God's will for our family."

If a husband doesn't want his wife to go to church at all, it's possible that a wife's willingness to honor her husband's request of her may help draw him closer to God. If he sees you are not putting church in front of him, the marriage may be strengthened and a husband could eventually soften and encourage his wife to go to church. Sometimes the husband will even go with his wife to a church where he feels welcomed after he sees that she was willing to honor his request to stay home. Perhaps there is another time during the week when a wife can go to a Bible study that may be okay with her husband, or an online Christian group she can participate in. Of course, you don't put your husband above God in your life, but there may be seasons when you show your husband that he is more important than attending a particular church service or a particular church. God may change a husband's heart when a wife is willing to make this sacrifice for a time. This would be something about which to fervently pray and seek God's leading. There can also be seasons when a husband simply asks his wife to scale back how much time she is spending at church, because he feels that the marriage or family is suffering. A wife would wisely seek to cut down on her activities at church in that situation whether her husband is a believer or not. Yes, teaching a class or singing in the choir is wonderful. But those things are not as important as your marriage covenant and your primary ministry to your husband.

THROUGH SEXUAL INTIMACY

God designed marriage and sex to be beautiful and good. If disrespect or control has been a primary factor in a husband's lack of sexual desire, God often heals and restores our marriages in this area over time when we are willing to do things His way. When God designed men, women, masculinity, femininity, marriage, romance, sex, and family, He did so wisely. When He gives us commands about marriage, it is for our protection and benefit in every area of our lives. God wired men to respond to the respect, admiration, and trust of their wives. He wired us to feel attracted to our husbands when we respect them and honor them, too. It's a win-win! I have seen this time and time again. When a wife begins to obey God, learns to respect her husband, and relinquishes control, sexual intimacy often heats up in the following months or years. It makes total sense!

> "When [God] gives us commands
> about marriage, it is for our protection
> and benefit in every area of our lives."

Of course, there are sometimes circumstances beyond our control (medical, geographical, or mental health issues; sinful addictions; or other spiritual issues) that can cause us not to have fulfilling sex lives for a season or sometimes longer. Thankfully, even in those difficult times, we can experience the sufficiency of Christ and find peace, joy, and fulfillment in Him. If this topic is particularly painful for you, or there are medical problems or issues over which you have no control, this chapter may be a difficult one. Prayerfully consider when and if it is wise to read about this subject, my precious sister! I don't want to cause unnecessary pain for my sisters who are already hurting deeply.

Of course every couple's marriage is unique, so there will be different results and different timetables for everyone. It is very rare for both the husband and wife to always have the same level and intensity of sexual desire. There must be grace, unconditional love, and respect even more so in this area than in others, in my view. No matter which spouse feels neglected and which one feels smothered, these sexual issues can be extremely painful.

Some General Suggestions About Respect and Sex

Too much aggression or too much passivity can be a turn off for husbands. An admiring, responsive wife is generally a huge turn on for a man. As you begin to implement respect, you may see your husband desire you more sexually in time (unless there are other issues impacting his libido). Consider these suggestions:

- Do not criticize or insult his sexuality or manliness.
- Do not complain about your experience with him.
- Don't demand sex.
- Don't ridicule him, put him down, or humiliate him.
- Don't purposely withhold sex.
- Don't compare him to another man, real or fictional.
- Don't act like sex is a burden or a chore.
- Don't refuse him unless there is serious illness, pain, or an emergency of some sort (1 Cor. 7:3–5).
- Be excited to be with him and respond positively to what you like.
- Appreciate his desire for you.
- Smile at him.
- Look at him with desire if he is receptive to your sexual attention.
- Do things for him that you know bring him pleasure.
- Be confident in your own skin.
- Allow him to enjoy looking at your body, with lingerie or without, whichever he prefers most. (Keep in mind that some husbands are more visual than others.)

When He Doesn't Seem Interested

For the wife whose husband doesn't seem interested in physical intimacy as often as you would like, you are not alone! Many other wives are in this boat, too. I know that it doesn't seem that way when you read a lot of marriage books, but there are many marriages where the wife has the higher sex drive. That doesn't always mean there is a problem in the marriage or a problem with your husband.

Here are some things to prayerfully consider that have worked for some other wives:

- Possibly stop initiating altogether for a few weeks.
- Drop your expectations and stop exerting pressure.
- If he initiates, be responsive and appreciative.
- Examine your motives. Are you seeking to find your source of identity, acceptance, and love in your husband's willingness to have sex with you? Sex in marriage can be a wonderful blessing, but only Christ can meet our deepest emotional and spiritual needs.
- Try journaling when you are frustrated. Rip up the page if no one else should read it later.
- Appreciate anything your man does do for you.
- Don't accuse him of being homosexual. That is *major* disrespect to your husband! (If he shows a number of signs that he is attracted to men, please seek appropriate godly, experienced, wise counsel.)
- Don't automatically assume he must be having an affair if he has a lower drive than you do.
- Focus on being content with what he is willing to give you as you find true contentment in Christ alone.

Many husbands need weeks, months, or even years to feel safe enough to take down their walls. They want to see that we are not just changing for a few hours, but for the rest of our lives. It can take time—a long time—for them to trust us again. We are going to have to be willing to obey God and wait as long as it takes, even though it can be hard and painful.

When You're Not Interested

If you aren't interested in having physical intimacy with your husband as often as he would like, you are also not alone! Here are some ideas that have worked for some other wives:

- Tell him you want to have time with him and thank him for desiring you.
- Give him ideas of things that might help increase your libido.
- Be sure to tell him when he does things you like.
- Flirt back with him, responding graciously and joyfully.
- If you can't be available, tell him how much you want to be with him and plan a time (preferably the next morning or the next night).
- If he has hygiene issues that turn you off, say something in a pleasant tone of voice like, "If you take care of X, I am all yours."
- Be willing to talk to your doctor quickly if you are dealing with medical issues or pain. Show your husband that keeping your sex life vibrant and healthy is a priority to you, even when there are problems.
- Be willing to receive godly counseling if you were sexually abused or molested in the past and sex is a difficult thing for you because of those deep wounds and emotional scars.
- Realize that for him, sex may be the way he bonds most with you emotionally and spiritually.
- Let him be himself and have needs that are different from yours without being "wrong."
- Enjoy getting to know him. Ask him about his sexual desires and appetite. Explore what it is like to live in his mind and to have his masculine perspective and needs.

About Financial Matters

Although there is not one right way for all couples to manage finances, there are some general principles that I believe can be very helpful as we seek to honor our husbands and God regarding financial issues. Everything we have comes from God. We are simply stewards of what God has allowed us to manage. Proverbs has much to say about not being in debt, spending wisely, and honoring God with our money. Jesus also addresses the issue of money many times, and so does the entire New Testament. We would do well to study what Scripture teaches about finances and to study wise teaching about handling finances. A Dave Ramsey financial course may be very helpful (see http://www.daveramsey.com).

We can honor God and our husbands by sticking to the family budget and not overspending. We can let our husbands know before we make large purchases. We can also seek to avoid being super controlling and restrictive on our husbands, dictating to them exactly what they can and can't spend. If a wife is handling the finances but feels that she must often ask her husband not to spend so much or fears that she may be too controlling or too overwhelmed with the finances, perhaps she may want to relinquish finances to her husband. Sometimes this helps a man take more responsibility when he sees exactly what is coming in and going out. (If your husband has significant learning disabilities, ADD, bipolar disorder, or gambling addictions, this arrangement may not be best for your marriage. Please seek God's wisdom for your situation.) Some husbands prefer for their wives to do the actual bookkeeping, but the husband helps make the budget and helps to make big decisions. He supervises and the wife may think of herself as the "secretary," in a sense. Ideally both spouses would have access to the financial accounts and transparency so that no one is hiding spending or debt. I also believe both spouses need to have input into deciding on the budget and sharing concerns they have. I also like the idea of having a joint bank account so that the money is "ours," rather than "yours" and "mine."

For wives who make more money than their husbands or who are the sole breadwinners, this area has many extra temptations. It is easy to think that if we make more money, we should control everything in the marriage, so we may have to guard against this tendency. And if we are the sole breadwinners, there will be greater temptation than ever for a wife to disrespect her husband's leadership. I am not saying that it would never be God's will for a wife to be the only financial support for the family. Sometimes it is unavoidable for many reasons. Or perhaps a couple believes this is what God desires them to do. But if this is the situation, I believe a wife will need to do much praying and seeking God to look for very special ways to continue to acknowledge her husband as the leader in the home and to focus on respecting him with extra diligence.

AROUND EXTENDED FAMILY AND OTHERS

Relationships with extended family can get very complicated. Some parents tend to expect their children to maintain allegiance and submission to them as they did when they were young. But there is a new covenant when a marriage is formed, so there must be new loyalties. Our ultimate respect and submission is to God first, then to our husbands. You have a covenant with your husband, not your parents. If you are forced to choose, you must show your husband that you are on his team, even if it leads to difficult relationships with other family members. This will strengthen your marriage and empower your husband to protect, lead, and guide you in the way God intends him to.

So they are no longer two, but one flesh. Therefore what God has joined together, let no one separate." (Matt. 19:6)

> "There is a new covenant when a marriage is formed, so there must be new loyalties. . . . You have a covenant with your husband, not your parents."

Kari's Story

I don't know how to fully describe the horror we lived for so many years with my husband's family, . . . which led to a chasm between my husband and myself. . . . We started fighting with each other because I was so hurt and wanted reconciliation. He was bent on being mad at me that I could let them hurt me, and said they were unwilling to change or grow in maturity to Christ, so it was time to shut down the relationships. He wanted to close up the doors to inviting further interaction and hurt. I finally let him lead and I submitted to his requests. . . . In six months, things got worse than they had ever been and many things came to a head. At last, some real communication, apologies, and healing took place in some of the relationships. This was a big deal. Six more months passed, and my husband made the decision that he wasn't ready to lift all the boundaries. He decided that our family would not be attending the next holiday event. I battled this in my heart. I felt like it was the wrong choice. . . . I thought he was selfish and making an ungodly choice out of pride. But I obeyed his leadership. . . . Eventually, my husband agreed to attend some family events and allowed the kids to interact with his family again. Things are not perfect . . . but my willingness to listen to my husband led to healthy change of many of the relationships and our ability to have interaction with his family instead of continuing in a direction that was leading to complete severance of all communication. The fact that I respected my husband in that huge decision did two things. First, it brought us closer together because I trusted my husband to lead in the situation and he saw that I was willing to follow him, making him more courageous to make decisions in the future. Second, it helped me gain perspective that not everything has to go my way for me to be happy and able to move on in life. . . . His way is working better than the way I forced us to try for so many years.

A Buffet of Suggestions

Here are some suggestions for you to consider to honor your husband at family get-togethers. These are different ideas to try or to prayerfully think about. They are not rules and they won't all apply in every situation. Ultimately, it is up to you to listen carefully to God's voice and your husband's leadership in each particular situation.

- Smile and look at your husband when he is talking and listen to him with interest.
- Give him the freedom to decide what he wants to do, what he wants to eat, to whom he wishes to speak, etc.
- Ask for what you want with a pleasant, friendly tone of voice. For example, "I'd love for you to sit with us in the other room for awhile." Then be gracious no matter what he chooses to do.
- Praise him genuinely in front of others at appropriate times (not constantly but one or two heart-felt sentences during the day about things about which you are proud of him would be great).
- Treat your husband's family with great respect and honor. Don't criticize them or your husband may feel he has to defend his family against you—not a good way to increase intimacy in your marriage. If you do disrespect his family, your husband will likely feel that you have stepped out from under his protection and covering and that you are on your own. How can he defend you if you are in the wrong?
- If there are people who verbally attack you in the extended family, stay in the same room as your husband. Most likely, these people will only attack you if they can get you alone.
- Seek not to disrespect him in any way in front of others.

- If people want you to commit your family to something, check with your husband first, or if he is there, look at him, smile, and let him answer (unless you have agreed together that you will handle the schedule).
- If a particular family member refuses to allow your husband to come to his or her house, it may be best if you don't go either, unless your husband suggests otherwise. No need to create a big fuss. Just simply and sweetly say something like, "Okay, I understand. But if my husband isn't welcome and respected in your home, then my children and I are not going to be able to come. Thanks for the offer."
- If a family member of yours disrespects your husband and your husband is not there, gently but firmly say, "Please do not disrespect my husband." Or "Please do not speak about my husband like that."
- If your husband is disrespected and he is there, check first to see if he prefers to handle the situation himself. He may not want to feel that you are coming to his rescue. This will depend on your husband, and perhaps whether it is your family or his family doing the disrespecting.
- Be content with him and what you have.
- Don't compare your husband to others.
- Don't try to force your husband into doing something he doesn't want to do.

THE RESULTS OF DISRESPECTING MY HUSBAND

I wish that I had thought through my disrespectful approach to my husband the first summer we got married. I didn't even know I was being disrespectful then, but a wife's disrespect repels her husband, destroys intimacy, and creates tension, competition, and strife. I wanted greater intimacy and connection, which were good desires, but I was doomed to fail because I took the wrong path to approach my husband with my needs and concerns. It is important for us to evaluate the path we choose, to see where that path ends before we choose it.

If I decide to criticize or disrespect my husband, I will probably get some of the following results:

- He will probably not want to be close to me again for a while on multiple levels.
- He will probably not feel safe being vulnerable with me.
- He will lose respect for me.
- He will lose trust and faith in me.
- His spiritual confidence and willingness to lead and love well may be shaken.
- His spirit may be crushed, or he may feel depressed and discouraged.
- He may resent me.
- Our spiritual, emotional, mental, and physical intimacy may be damaged.
- He may feel defeated and like a failure as a man.
- Satan may get a foothold in our marriage.

I think if we consider a controlling or disrespectful woman in our own lives and how we feel when we have to interact with her, it may help us have empathy for how our husbands may feel if we act in those ways. When a woman is very critical of you and tries to dictate things to you (whether she is your mom, your mother-in-law, a sister, or a coworker), do you naturally feel all warm and fuzzy toward her? Or do you think to yourself, "How can I get away from her as quickly as possible?" What do you think when this woman calls you or walks in the door? No one likes to feel controlled or disrespected. We all long to feel loved, respected, accepted, cherished, and adored. For a beautiful example of a godly wife, and the power she has to bless her husband and family, please check out Proverbs 31 sometime.

Disrespect may seem like a small thing to us as women today, but to husbands it is a very big thing. Perhaps you would like to ask your guy some general questions: "Do husbands need respect from their wives?" Or, "If a husband feels disrespected by his wife, what does that do to him as a man?" Maybe he would be open to you asking, "What are some things wives do that would be disrespectful or respectful to a husband?" It will be interesting to find out what your husband thinks about the importance of a wife avoiding disrespect. I encourage you to have your antennae up this week to notice the interactions between men and women around you and even in the media to see if you can decode what behaviors, words, and attitudes from women might convey disrespect to men and which things might convey genuine respect. Look for women who seem to understand respect and watch how they speak and act around their husbands or even around other men. Watch the way men interact with respectful women. Notice the results of interactions when women treat men with disrespect, contempt, disdain, ridicule, and negativity. Watch how the men respond, and prayerfully consider what messages you would most like to send to your husband to bless and build up your marriage.

Communicating Our Desires Respectfully

Before we can begin to communicate respectfully, it is important for us to decide what things are productive to share and what things would be destructive. Respect is about much more than just how we say something. The words and tone of voice we use are part of respect. But as we grow, real respect involves *respectful motives* and *respectful self-talk* in our hearts, which requires total heart change in order to do authentically. I could say something in a respectful way, but if I harbor disrespect in my heart, I am not truly respecting Greg or obeying God. God can give us His power and wisdom to filter our words through Scripture so that we can discard sinful thoughts that might hurt and destroy our husbands and our marriages. The earlier we can catch destructive thoughts, the better! Over time (many months or even several years), God changes our thought patterns and desires so that eventually, we don't usually even think the disrespectful things anymore.

I used to think that being myself meant I should be able to share any and every thought that ever crossed my mind. But God reminds us that, "Sin is not ended by multiplying words, but the prudent hold their tongues" (Prov. 10:19). Another way I have heard this worded is, "When words are many, sin is not absent." I always used to hate that verse—probably because I talked quite a lot. One of the first steps toward godly wisdom for those who have been rather outspoken is to move toward more silence, especially when we want to say something that could be sinful, hurtful, or negative. This doesn't mean you will need to be totally silent. But if most of your words have involved sinful motives and sinful content, you may be pretty quiet for a long time while you figure out what else to talk about. I sure was. In time, you will probably need to move toward more talking until you find the right balance of quantity and content that honors God. If you are a woman who tends to be "too quiet," you probably don't have to focus on speaking less to avoid sin. For you, the greater challenge may be to recognize what your thoughts are and then to have the courage and wisdom about what to say and how to best share with others.

> *Lord,*
> *Speak directly to my heart. Help me to hear Your voice and truth clearly. Let me learn to recognize the enemy's voice as I learn about guarding my thoughts and words. Purify me so that I might become the woman You call me to be for Your glory. Make me holy as You are holy. Help me to use my words to bring life, not harm, in my marriage.*
> *In the name and power of Christ, amen!*

SOMETIMES SILENCE IS GOLDEN

There are many verses about the wisdom of silence in Proverbs: "Even fools are thought wise if they keep silent, and discerning if they hold their tongues" (Prov. 17:28). For those who are seeking to become more godly women, I believe that this is the place we must start in our understanding of wholesome, beneficial, godly conversations with people. I have noticed that if I feel extremely compelled to share something right away that is negative, I need to carefully evaluate whether I am listening to my sinful self, the enemy, or God. God can prompt me to share something quickly at times. But, when my sinful nature is in control, it seems more like an undeniable urge to blurt out what I think is so important as soon as possible, not taking into account whether I might offend or hurt someone.

In general, silence, even wrongful silence, tends to do a lot less damage to others than words wrongly spoken. It can feel like we are not being ourselves at first when we begin to censor our words. But we have died to our old selves, if we are in Christ. Now we are seeking to be our new selves in Jesus. We are free to share all of ourselves as new creations in Christ and to be that new Holy Spirit–filled self all the time around everyone (2 Cor. 5:17). Good news! I don't have to censor the good things God does in my heart and life. I will need to choose what to share, when to share, and how to share wisely. But I don't have to be afraid of my husband finding out what I really think because I have nothing to hide when the Spirit is in charge and my thoughts are pure and honoring to Christ. If Greg finds out what I said about him to my friend or what I wrote about him in my prayer journal, I am not usually concerned now like I used to be when I said negative things about him to other people and tore him apart in my journal on a daily basis. There is so much peace in knowing that in my thinking and talking about my husband, I have been respectful.

> "When God's Spirit is in control, we can begin to recognize temptation very quickly and shoot down destructive ideas before we allow them to take root in our hearts and before we act on them."

Our being more and more holy and godly will eventually become normal. Then our old sinful ways will start to feel foreign and even repulsive. When God's Spirit is in control, we can begin to recognize temptation very quickly and shoot down destructive ideas before we allow them to take root in our hearts and before we act on them. Jesus gives us the power to live in victory over sin each day. We may stumble at times and we won't achieve sinless perfection until we reach heaven. But in Christ, we can grow greatly in maturity and walk in victory as a normal habit, not because we are so good, but because Jesus is so good and His power is flooding our hearts. This has nothing to do with our strength, following rules, or trying harder; it has everything to do with us allowing God's Spirit total access to our hearts, minds, and lives.

> Set a guard over my mouth, LORD; keep watch over the door of my lips. (Ps. 141:3)

If a husband has felt very smothered, disrespected, or controlled for many months or years, he may need some extra silence at first. I picture it as if a husband's soul has been "sunburned" if he has felt quite disrespected for a while. He may tend to be extra sensitive to anything that could remotely sound disrespectful as he heals. Sometimes once a husband feels respected and safe again, a wife can have freedom to share about more topics. So some extra silence may be a temporary phase until a wife learns greater discretion and her husband heals. Different husbands have different personalities, too. So a more introverted man, who recharges his energy by being alone, may need more silence even once he feels safe and respected than a more extroverted man, who gets energized from being around people.

When You Have Sinful Motives

When I have sinful motives, it is definitely a good time to remain silent. I already know what the outcome will be if my flesh is in control: contention, misunderstandings, hurt feelings, loss of intimacy, and destruction. I might just want to be with Greg, which is not wrong in and of itself, but when I am not filled with God's Spirit, I become desperate and needy in my communication of my needs and in my response if he doesn't do what I want him to do.

The sinful motive I struggle with most is my pride. If I look at myself as being so much more spiritual than Greg and I look down on him as being a bigger sinner than I am, my pride can easily lead to other wrong motives and sinful thoughts. For instance, if I believe I am better than my husband, then I will have a tough time respecting him. If I don't respect him, I sure won't want to submit to his leadership. I may begin to look on him with contempt and resentment, all the while believing I am totally justified.

Some other sinful motives that are a big red flag to me not to speak at the moment:

- If I feel compelled to interrogate and accuse my husband of wrongdoing, as if I am a prosecuting attorney examining him on the witness stand in court
- If I want to share something with my husband about someone else that would hurt the other person or could be considered gossip
- If I want to gossip about my husband to someone else or share something about him that would hurt him or make him feel betrayed by me
- If I want to try to change my husband and force him to do something so that I can get what I want from him
- If I am feeling really disappointed in my husband for not meeting my expectations. This may or may not involve sinful thoughts, but I can quickly spiral downward from here if I am not careful
- If I am focusing on all of the bad things in my husband and can't see any good things
- If I am thinking things like, "He should do X for me" and "I deserve Y"
- If I am seeking my will above God's will

- If I am complaining about something
- If I want to argue

I am not saying I should never address issues with my husband if I find these motives in my heart. But I do need to take these motives to God and repent of them, if necessary, and have things in order in my soul and with God before attempting to address an issue with my husband, according to Matthew 7:1–5.

When You Aren't Sure Whether to Speak

If I am not sure if I should talk about something, I have learned that it is often best to wait.[1] There can be exceptions in cases of emergencies or when a very important decision must be made quickly. But if an issue can wait and I am not completely at peace about whether I should address it, I personally like to journal my thoughts and pray first. I like to write out all of my thoughts, emotions, and concerns to help me determine if my negative feelings are a flag to some sinful motive in my heart, or whether I am being sinned against by someone and need to address it, or whether I am just hormonal or tired. If I believe I need to share something, I want to wait to be sure that the timing is right and my motives are honorable toward God and Greg. If the thoughts and motives I write down are things that are sinful and might hurt someone else if they were to read it, I tear it up after I am done. (I shredded a lot of journal notes in the first few years of this journey.)

When I started my journey to become a godly wife, I knew that silence was the only way I could avoid speaking disrespectfully at first, especially since my mind and heart were still swirling with an ocean of disrespectful thoughts and motives. My journal and prayer life were my only outlet for several years. I have never gone back to my old ways of sharing all of my thoughts with any person. My deepest thoughts are still primarily just between God and me. I am not saying this is what every wife should do. But processing my thoughts in a private way in the light of God's Word helps me figure out exactly what I am thinking and gives me a safe place to carefully decide whether I should verbalize my ideas to Greg. This saves me from over-sharing with a friend, gossiping with a family member, or betraying my husband's confidence.

If you have a godly wife mentor with whom you can share your struggles and who will pray with you, that is wonderful! Now I also have some prayer partner ladies with whom I keep myself transparent. If I realize I am wrestling with a sinful thought, and I am still having problems after prayer, I make sure to share my temptation or struggle with Greg or my prayer partners. Isolating myself during temptation could make me easy prey for the enemy.

Unsolicited Advice

I have learned that I don't generally need to voice an opinion when my husband makes decisions for himself about what to eat, what to wear, how to manage his relationships with others, how to drive, how to spend his free time, how to handle problems at work, how to spend (or save) every dollar, how to relate to the children, and so on. Greg is a grown man, capable of making his own decisions. If he asks for my input, I can offer it humbly, in a friendly way. But unless my husband asks me for my counsel concerning a decision he makes for himself (I am not speaking about family decisions here, but his personal decisions), I can choose to honor his God-given right to make his own decisions and to face the natural consequences of those decisions. We both appreciate it when no one tries to micromanage our personal choices. Might I be adversely impacted if my husband chooses some unhealthy habits? Yes, that is possible. But Greg needs to have enough freedom to be his own person. If my husband has difficulty remembering to do something and asks me to assist him, then it is fine for me to give him a friendly reminder. In general, however, unsolicited advice often comes across as an attempt to control another person.

I can sometimes share my preferences about what I like for myself, if I can do this in a friendly way without attempting to pressure or manipulate him. If I say, "I think I'll order baked chicken. I don't really like to eat more than about three ounces of red meat per week," with a pleasant tone of voice, that would probably be fine. But this same statement could easily turn into manipulation or condemnation if I say it in a condescending way, like I really think Greg should have the same conviction about red meat that I do. In that case, it would be better for me not to share that particular piece of trivia about my dietary preferences. I can test my motives by asking myself:

- Am I sharing in a friendly, pleasant way just so he knows more about me?
- Am I trying to make him change because my way is better?

There are times when I can share suggestions or requests. But it is really critical that when he makes a choice with which I do not agree, I respond with grace, not with contempt, pressure, or resentment. In Christ, I can choose to be content no matter what Greg chooses to do (Phil. 4:12–13). The longer I have been respectful, the more open my husband's heart and mind will probably be to me sharing ideas about many topics. I can share what I want to do about our children's nutrition. I can share ideas I am considering for my own nutrition. I can seek to cook healthy meals for my family. But my husband doesn't need or want me to be his mother. He wants me to be his wife. He would appreciate it if I respect that there are many areas where he can make decisions for himself and I can make decisions for myself.

If I am genuinely concerned about Greg's health or his diet, I can prayerfully consider whether God might want me to approach him about these things and then say something like, "I love being your wife. I really want us to be together for as long as possible. I know that God is sovereign over our lives and that He knows the number of our days. I trust Him completely. I also know that there are real consequences to the choices we make. It would give me so much peace of mind to know that your body is healthy. I feel really sad at the thought of something happening to you that maybe could have been prevented." I do not believe that me attempting to monitor and direct my husband's every dietary choice, or other personal choices, will bless him, motivate him to make healthier choices, or increase intimacy in our marriage. In fact, my attempting to micromanage his daily choices would probably decrease intimacy between us because my husband would likely feel smothered. I don't believe that respecting my husband means I should "enable" an addiction or harmful behavior. If my husband had diabetes, I don't think I would want to buy him sugary treats. If he had an addiction to alcohol, I wouldn't buy alcohol for him. If he has a porn addiction and wants me to watch that with him, I would have to refuse.

If a husband is very sick or injured and says he's fine, but his wife knows that he desperately needs emergency medical attention, I vote to call an ambulance even if he says not to. Of course, if a husband is harming himself or genuinely endangering others, a wife will need to take action and seek appropriate outside help.

When the Flesh Is Weak

There are certain times when I know I need to use extra caution if I think that I should share something, especially something negative, with Greg. When I have low blood sugar or am hormonal, exhausted, sick, in pain, rushing to get somewhere, or overwhelmed and stressed with all I have to do, these times will be most tempting to blurt something out without really thinking through what I am saying. When my flesh is weak, I run low on my own strength and patience. I need to depend more than ever on God's power in these moments.

I think it is important for me to let Greg know when I am experiencing health problems or am in a weakened state in my flesh. He needs to know that I need food soon, that I am extremely sleep deprived, that I am hurting physically, that I am dealing with PMS, or whatever the situation is. Keeping this kind of information to myself could be disrespectful or even dangerous. If I am so sleep deprived that I know it is not safe for me to drive, I make sure to let my husband know. I may have to say "I really wish I could do that for you, but right now, I just can't physically manage that" to some things that he asks me to do when I am having significant health problems. I can share my issue with Greg once and that will usually be enough. If things change, I might want to let him know. If I have a chronic medical problem (and I do have a number of them), I can share about it when it is particularly troublesome or there is something important that I believe Greg needs to know. I am careful not to slip into complaining, where I just repeat my problems over and over even after Greg is aware of them and the situation is not an emergency.

Another time I need to use a great deal of caution before I speak is if I have not had the time I need with God each day. If I am drifting from God or not closely connected to Him, I can crash and burn quickly. I seriously cannot do anything good apart from God. I have to have at least thirty to sixty minutes per day in Bible reading and fervent, focused prayer. If I go for a few days without that spiritual intimacy with God, or if I begin to cherish sin in my heart, I start to operate in my own power again and can begin to miss signs of temptation and lose the power of His Spirit. I know that I am always completely capable of any kind of sin if I am far enough away from God. The only good that is in me is all from Jesus; none of it is my own goodness. I need to remember this truth with great humility and always acknowledge my total dependence upon Christ. I have to abide in Christ so that His power flows into me (John 15:1–8). I try to wait to have any major discussions until after some quality time with God, when my spirit has been renewed.

Luke 6:45

> "If I go for a few days without that spiritual intimacy with God, or if I begin to cherish sin in my heart, I start to operate in my own power again and can begin to miss signs of temptation and lose the power of His Spirit."

I also want to use more discretion when my husband's flesh is weak or if he is facing a great disappointment or trial in his life. I know that Greg may need some extra rest and emotional or physical space during some of these situations. Some husbands desire more attention and affection when they are stressed or sick. If a husband is not a believer or is struggling in his faith, words about spiritual things will probably not have a beneficial impact (1 Peter 3:1–2). In such circumstances, God commands a wife to show respect and honor as she lives out godly attitudes, speech, and behavior without preaching at her husband. God knows this approach will speak much more powerfully to a husband who is hurting spiritually. We will need to be very sensitive to God's Spirit to know exactly what to do. You may think your husband is far from God, but you could be wrong and you could be misjudging him. God knows your husband's heart; you do not. Silence in this situation may prevent a husband from feeling criticized and condemned, and will help provide a more favorable atmosphere for his spiritual healing and growth.

An Emotional Avalanche

When my flesh is weak, I may be greatly tempted to vent my frustrations to my husband or *at* my husband. I may think that I need to unleash all of my negative emotions so that I can feel better. The problem is, I might feel better after lashing out at him, or "emotionally vomiting" all over him, as Nina Roesner describes it in her blog, The Respect Dare,[2] but what does my outburst do to my husband? Does it build intimacy, connection, and trust, or does it repel my husband, making him feel unsafe around me because I seem to be emotionally out of control? If I choose to send my husband a three- to four-thousand-word email—or if I spend an hour or two talking at him—blasting him with all of my anger, sadness, disappointment, and frustration in great detail, he will probably be pretty overwhelmed by the sheer volume of words and the intensity of my negative emotions. He also may not be able to determine what I need from him. He may do better if I just cut to the chase. Greg explained to me that he often felt like I was a "verbal firing squad" when I emotionally vomited on him, and all he wanted to do was run for cover. Other men describe feeling like they are drowning in an "ocean of negative emotions" and like they need to try to swim for shore to get away. Greg can hear me and care about my needs and feelings when I adjust my delivery and approach. I can still communicate what I need to, but I will do it in a way that Greg can receive well.

When You Want to Share a Critical Comment About Something Minor

If I want to say something to Greg about a matter that is small in the grand scheme of life, it could be wise to hold my tongue. What does it really matter if he takes the route home that can sometimes take a few more minutes? Of course, if I am having some kind of medical emergency, I may implore him to take the fastest route. But under normal circumstances, I can be peaceful and content as Greg makes his own decisions about how to drive. I can choose to enjoy the trip and savor his company as I trust him to get us safely to our destination. My particular husband is a very intelligent, capable, and responsible man. I can also refrain from saying anything if my husband is telling a story and he gets a minor detail wrong. Does it matter that much that an event took place on a Tuesday rather than a Wednesday? My husband may enjoy the freedom of telling his story himself without me chiming in to correct the little details. Of course, there may be times when he looks at me as he tries to remember a detail, and that would be a great opportunity for me to share.

I may also decide to say nothing if my husband handles a discipline situation with our children in a way that may not be exactly what I would have done. If he is not sinning against our children, and he is plugged in as a father, I don't have to step in and voice my opinion on every small issue. In fact, I prefer to thank him for taking care of our children, even if he uses different methods than I would. I demonstrate trust by not trying to micromanage or supervise all of my husband's choices. I can respect him by giving him space to be different from me without trying to make him feel that he is wrong.

SOMETIMES SHARING IS VITAL

There are countless things that wives can and should share with their husbands. I know it can seem like there is a lot of territory that is off limits to us when we begin to learn about respecting our husbands and honoring God with our speech and our thoughts. Thankfully, as we grow, it becomes obvious that there are boundaries, but there are also a lot of new ways to share. I don't know any reasonable husband who wants his wife to share nothing, think nothing, have no opinions of her own, always agree with him, and contribute nothing to the marriage relationship from her own mind, heart, and soul. That would be a very sick marriage.

When You Want to Use Your Words to Give Life and Blessing

For wives who have not struggled with disrespect and who were possibly too passive, too quiet, or "too respectful" before, this may be your starting point. Now it is time to find the courage and strength to share more things with your husband. One of the first things I learned to do was to voice my appreciation about the good I saw in Greg. Words don't do as much for Greg as they do for me. Some husbands love a lot of words and details. For Greg, a simple sentence or two of appreciation per day or per week can be a blessing. Honestly, my attitude, behavior, and motives mattered a lot more to Greg than these kinds of respectful words, but learning to use my words for good is part of this process. I learned to express my gratitude whenever Greg did something I liked. When I noticed something I admired about Greg, I mentioned it briefly and freely. I focused my thoughts on Philippians 4:8 things. I also daily wrote down all the good things I could think of about Greg and my life, as well. So it became more and more natural for me to start to voice these things upon which I was meditating daily.

> Finally, brothers and sisters, whatever is true, whatever is noble, whatever is right, whatever is pure, whatever is lovely, whatever is admirable—if anything is excellent or praiseworthy—think about such things. (Phil. 4:8)

This is so key: whatever I think about in my mind and meditate upon in my heart is what will come out of my mouth. My thoughts also become my personal reality in many ways and color my understanding of my husband and my marriage. Good thoughts cause me to think and feel good things and contribute good words, attitudes, and actions to my marriage. Bad thoughts cause me to think and feel bad things and contribute bad words, attitudes, and actions to my marriage.

"This is so key: whatever I think about in my mind and meditate upon in my heart is what will come out of my mouth."

> A good man brings good things out of the good stored up in his heart, and an evil man brings evil things out of the evil stored up in his heart. For the mouth speaks what the heart is full of. (Luke 6:45)

Some people think that I endorse women being fake, "Stepford wives" who paint an artificial smile on their faces and who quietly feign happiness while seething with negativity on the inside. That approach is doomed to fail because, eventually, a wife's real negative feelings will seep out or explode all over her husband. Whitewashing ungodly thinking cures nothing. This journey is about us cooperating with God to remove all of the toxic stuff from our minds, hearts, and souls, and it is about us having a new spirit that is being sanctified—made to be more and more holy and like Christ over time. If I am going to truly respect my husband, it cannot be an exercise in changing externals. I may start there, but as I learn and mature, God empowers me to cultivate genuine respect and godliness by carefully monitoring my thoughts. I must have the discipline, through the Holy Spirit's power, to shoot down any disrespectful, bitter, or sinful thoughts in my heart immediately, and to purposely replace them with God's truth and genuinely respectful thoughts. There will be times when I must share hard things. But in God's design, I can do that and maintain my respect for Greg and my cooperative spirit. I am almost always free in my marriage to express good things: my genuine joy, praise for my husband, thanksgiving, peace, respect, honor, friendliness, affection, appreciation, praise for God, and my good thoughts as God leads me to—the major exception being if my husband is not a believer, then I will probably not talk about God, the Bible, or spiritual things to him (1 Peter 3:1–6).

When You Believe God Is Prompting You

When you are walking in close intimacy with Christ and you are living in the power of His Spirit, He may nudge you to say something particular at a certain time or to remain quiet. He may burden your heart to pray. He may ask you to be still before Him for a time. He may give you ideas about ways to show honor and respect to your husband that will specifically bless him. What an incredible treasure to have the

voice of God's Spirit whispering in our ears. This is what we all desperately need in order to be the women God calls us to be!

> Whether you turn to the right or to the left, your ears will hear
> a voice behind you, saying, "This is the way; walk in it." (Isa.
> 30:21)

I can remember one evening when I was in our study by myself reading the Bible and writing in my prayer journal. I was upset that my
family wasn't spending as much time in prayer and Bible reading as
I thought we should. Suddenly, I very clearly heard God speak to my
heart, "Stop reading your Bible and go watch TV with Greg and your
children." I started to argue, "But, Lord, I want to be here with You!"
He impressed upon my heart again, "Go be with your family and spend
time with them." I decided to obey.

I have noticed that often what God prompts me to do is not what I
would naturally think to do on my own. Many times, God has prompted
me how and when to share a concern I had with Greg. I can hear Him
saying, "This is the time. Here are the points to humbly, gently share,
then let Me take it from there." I can recognize His prompting because it
is usually calm and I feel peaceful; it is very different from that panicked,
urgent feeling of the flesh screaming that I need to blurt out something
that may be hurtful. I do want to use caution here. It is possible that we
can deceive ourselves sometimes and think we are hearing God's voice
when we are really listening to ourselves or to the enemy. We must be
willing to "test the spirits" (1 John 4:1); if something we think God is
prompting us to do goes against God's Word, we must reject that nudging and cling to the Word of God as our primary source of truth.

When You Want to Connect Emotionally

God gave emotions as a gift to humanity. I believe it is a good thing
for us to communicate the entire range of our emotions with our

husbands. We can share feelings without blaming our husbands for the bad ones. We can be vulnerable, authentic, and real as we also respect and honor God and our husbands.

I like Laura Doyle's method in *The Surrendered Wife*[3] of simply stating feelings, emotions, and desires without blame or elaborate detail. For example:

- I feel sad about this.
- I feel nervous.
- I feel afraid.
- I feel angry about X.
- I am really frustrated about this situation.
- I feel completely overwhelmed.

The beauty of us sharing simple feelings is that our husbands can hear us because these statements are digestible and concise. This approach is nonthreatening and honest. It is difficult to argue with someone's emotions. They are what they are and only that person can know what he or she is feeling. There are times when one simple statement about what you are feeling is powerful enough. Other times, you may share a bit more. Maybe when your husband says, "What are you nervous about?" then you may go into more details. But instead of taking an hour or two to tell him, he may appreciate a summary. If he wants more information, he will probably ask. Or, if you realize you left out something truly important, you can share that as well. This allows me to communicate the most important information about my feelings in a way that draws Greg closer to me rather than repelling him. I have so much more power and "voice" now than I ever had when I spent hours explaining my negative thoughts and feelings. I make a statement or share for a few minutes. Greg understands my heart and my needs and I feel more connected. He can decide how he wants to respond without feeling condemned, pressured, coerced, or threatened. And this takes so much less time and less of an emotional toll on both of us than my old way.

I believe it is important to share our positive emotions, as well. "I am so happy right now just getting to be with you!" "My heart is overflowing with thankfulness today." "I love being your wife!" When your husband gets to see all of your emotions and you present them in a gentle, feminine way, your feelings bless your marriage and increase emotional intimacy and connection. Your positive emotions make your husband feel like your hero. And when you express your negative emotions in respectful, concise ways, your husband also can choose to be your hero when possible, even in your struggles and frustrations.

> "When your husband gets to see all of your emotions and you present them in a gentle, feminine way, your feelings bless your marriage and increase emotional intimacy and connection."

Sometimes we may just want to talk through our feelings to process them. In that case, it can be helpful for us to share exactly what we need because our husbands often don't have the same kinds of needs to talk and emotionally connect that we do. For example, "I am not sure how I feel right now about this. It would help me so much if you would please listen to me for about five to ten minutes while I talk through things. Talking is how I process my emotions. Just knowing you are listening is such a blessing to me and I will feel better after you listen to me." I think it would be great to let our husbands know we would like to hear their thoughts many times, too, and we can show our husbands that we value their input, wisdom, and leadership. Sometimes our men like to have the chance to implement a real solution to our problems, too, rather than just listening.

When Your Husband's Personal Choices Impact You

If my husband makes a decision that is actually a problem for me or causing a real hardship, like he is using cologne that I am allergic to, I want to share my needs and concerns with him. "Greg, I am so sorry, but I think that I may be allergic to your cologne." Or if my husband's snoring is keeping me awake, I may need to address the issue and ask for his cooperation so that I can sleep well. "Honey, I'm *so* sorry to bother you . . . but you are snoring and I can't sleep. I wonder if X might help? Thank you so much!" But if he tries a number of remedies and keeps snoring, then I may decide to go to another room to try to sleep. Or I might respectfully ask him if he would mind going to another room. I don't have to be silent if I really have a problem. I have the ability and the duty to share when I need help or need something to change.

When You Want to Share Your Needs or Desires

Men and women are all human beings, precious creations of God whose feelings, needs, and opinions matter, especially in marriage. Husbands and wives should be free to share their ideas, emotions, and desires. That doesn't mean we can always have things our way, but it is essential that we feel safe to share in ways that honor and respect others. I should be able to express myself without injuring Greg. He should be able to express himself without injuring me. Both of our ideas, perspectives, and personalities are important and we should both feel that we can be heard and that we have a voice. It can take time to get to this place and to heal, of course. I like Laura Doyle's approach about sharing our desires in a friendly yet straightforward way. There is no reason to try to manipulate or to pressure our husbands. We can simply share:

- I want to do X.
- I don't want to do Y.
- I like this.
- I don't like that.

I try to focus on suggestions and requests when I communicate with Greg rather than demands or directives. When I approach my husband, I use a pleasant tone of voice and a genuine smile, and say:

- I would really like to do this.
- It would mean so much to me if we could . . .
- I'm not sure I like that idea. What about if we did X, instead?
- Would you please do this for me when you get a chance?
- I could really use some help with Y.
- Do you have any ideas about how I might handle this problem?
- I have a problem. Would you be able to help me, please?
- I think I would prefer . . .
- Here is what I love about your idea . . . and here are a few thoughts I had that we might consider . . .
- I have been doing some thinking; would this be a good time for me to share my ideas?
- I have a few concerns that I would really like to share, if you don't mind.
- I think I may be confused. Would you please explain a bit more about your idea/plan? I want to be sure I completely understand.

Depending on your particular husband's personality, he may respond right away to your request or suggestion, or he may need time to think about what he wants to do before he is able to verbalize his ideas. Now instead of me hovering over Greg, expecting or demanding a response immediately, I casually walk into the room, smile at him, mention what I would like or what I need, then go about my business (unless something is an emergency). That way I don't pressure him. Some husbands might appreciate a few days' notice before having a deep talk about an important subject. "Honey, I'd like to talk about X this weekend. Just wanted to give you a heads up." I also keep in mind that Greg needs more time to process his thoughts and emotions than

I do with certain issues, so I allow him to be himself and take the time he needs. Be prepared to be gracious no matter what your husband's answer is to your idea. If he says "no" or "let's wait," use that time to pray, seek God, listen to God's promptings, and trust God's sovereignty to work things out for your ultimate good and His glory (Rom. 8:28). Thank your husband for his leadership even when he makes decisions you don't like, and remember that your husband will stand accountable to God for that decision, not you. If he says, "yes," thank him and show him that you greatly appreciate what he did for you.

HOW TO SHARE YOUR FEELINGS AND DESIRES RESPECTFULLY

The list below provides examples of how to respectfully share your feelings and desires with your husband. Remember, use a pleasant tone of voice and a smile, be casual (not pressuring him), and then give him time to think, if he needs it.

- Honey, I'd really like to think about homeschooling the children. I'm concerned about the ungodly influences they are exposed to in public school. I know you may have a different perspective about this. I'd love to talk about it sometime, maybe this weekend.
- I just found out that my favorite group is going to be in town next month. I would really like for us to go together. What do you think?
- I've been feeling overwhelmed trying to get the kids to bed on time lately. Do you have any suggestions about how I might handle that in a better way? (Or) I've been feeling overwhelmed trying to get the kids to bed on time lately. If you would help me by taking over story time, that would help me so much! Thank you! (Or) I need some help with the kids tonight, please. Would you read a story to them at 8:00 p.m.?
- (If he suggests sex and you are not in the mood) I would love to

be available to you. Maybe we can find a way to help me wind down a little bit. Then I am all yours. (Or) I am so sad! I'm not feeling well right now, but I want to be available as soon as possible. What if we set the alarm and try in the morning? (Or) What if I do X for you so that you can have release tonight? Then maybe we can be together "for real" as soon as possible? (Or) I am still feeling unsettled about what you said earlier. I want to be totally available to you sexually, but I need to know that this issue is resolved and that we are okay before I can feel trusting and open enough for sex. Maybe we could talk about that first and then make up?

- I am so excited for you about your new job opportunity out of state. What an honor that is! I have to admit, I feel really sad about the idea of leaving our home. I do have some concerns that I want to be sure we can talk about together as we make this decision. But, I want to support you however I can. If this is what you believe is best, I trust you and I will do everything I can to be joyful about it.
- Honey, would you start a load of whites in the washer sometime tonight, please? Thanks!
- (If he has hurt your feelings) That hurts my feelings. (Or) I feel sad when you talk to me like that. (Or) That tone of voice feels unloving to me. (Or) I really like it when you use a calm tone of voice with me. Then I can hear your heart so much more clearly. (Or) Please don't talk to me like that, honey.
- I'm feeling sad tonight but I know I would feel so much better if I get to cuddle with you for a while. I just can't be sad when you are holding me close.

Submitting Under Protest

One of the things I love most about learning to respect and honor Greg is that I no longer try to argue or fight with him. I love that we both feel heard, respected, valued, and cherished in all of our decisions. There is no need for raised voices. There is no need for anyone to feel attacked. We have the tools to handle disagreements calmly. Often, there isn't even any tension or loss of emotional connectedness even when we disagree. We both know that our marriage and oneness are much more important than the outcome of the decisions we make, so we can approach decisions as a team without fear that disagreement might destroy our marriage or wound someone.

> ## "I love that we both feel heard, respected, valued, and cherished in all of our decisions."

Once a wife has shared her thoughts with her husband and they realize that they cannot agree on an issue, one of my favorite ways a wife can communicate respectfully with her husband is to simply state that she does not agree with him, but will submit to him out of respect for his position. (I am talking about situations where the husband is not asking his wife to condone or commit sin, the husband is in his right mind, and there are no severe issues in the marriage.) A brother in Christ shared this concept with me, and I love it! There is no contention. There is no drama. There are no tears, most of the time. When a husband sees that his amazing, respectful wife, whom he greatly respects and dearly loves, sharply disagrees with him in an agreeable way, this will give him pause.

A believing husband knows that he is accountable to God for his decisions, and he will probably spend some extra time praying about a decision where his wife does not agree with him before proceeding. A wise husband will carefully weigh his wife's opposition to be sure he is not making a foolish decision and that what he wants to do is truly best in the sight of God for everyone in his family. Even if he is not a believer, a man will generally respond with great caution if his respectful, cooperative wife voices major concerns over the course of action he plans to take.

"Sweetheart, thank you for sharing what you believe we should do. You know, I have thought about it and prayed about this, and I really believe that this is not the best course of action for us. Thank you so much for listening to my perspective and concerns. If you believe that this is what is best for our family, I will submit to you 'under protest' in this situation. I can't agree with you, but I will cooperate with your decision, trust you, and pray for you. Thanks for your leadership, honey."

For a husband who is not a believer: "Babe, you have heard my thoughts about this decision. I have carefully listened to your thoughts. I still fully believe that this is *not* the right decision. But I will gladly honor your leadership and support you if you really believe this is what is best for us."

The Van Battery Incident

One morning right before we left for the beach, our minivan battery died. My husband, being the handy guy he is, jumped the van and got it going. I thanked him, smiled at him, and suggested pleasantly, "We have time to go by the auto parts store, if you want to, honey." He said, "No, I think we'll be fine." He thought the battery just got run down from having the doors open for a long time while we were packing the car. (Let me say here that a few years ago, I would have insisted that we check the battery. I would have worried constantly if we didn't check on it.) I decided to respect my husband's decision and said sincerely, in an upbeat tone, "Okay, whatever you think is best." Then I read my book and seriously didn't worry about it. This is the kind of peace God has given me daily for more than seven years now. By the time this incident happened, trusting God and my husband and respecting them was a normal, everyday thing because God had already done a lot of renovations in my mind and spirit. If I had actually been worried at the beginning of the trip, I could have said, "I would be able to relax and enjoy the trip a lot better if we could check the battery before we leave town, please." But I wasn't worried, so I didn't say that. We got to the condo at the beach and my husband parked the van. Later, Greg tried to crank up the van but the battery was dead. A few years ago, I would have berated him with an I-told-you-to-check-that-battery lecture and a lot of negative attitude. But God had been working in my heart about respecting my husband, so I didn't say anything negative. I didn't even think anything negative. I was totally calm and at peace. This was not really my problem. It was his. I knew he would take care of it. We were in an awkward parking place and our regular jumper cables would not work. I smiled at Greg sweetly with an I-know-you've-got-this-covered look and kept the kids quiet while he decided what to do. I read my book some more.

Within a few minutes, a man came over and asked my husband if we needed a jump. He had bought extra-long jumper cables a few weeks earlier. He said his wife had ridiculed him for bringing the cables on their trip and told him he would never need them. He insisted on bringing them just in case. He was our personal angel sent from God at exactly the right moment! He jumped our van. Greg thanked the man and went right to Wal-Mart and replaced the old battery. (I believe God nudged this husband to bring those cables. What a lesson for me to see that some little idea I think is silly might be God whispering to a husband.)

I didn't have to tell Greg what to do. I knew that God and Greg had things under control and there was no reason for me to get upset or worry. This was not a big deal. No one was in danger at any point. My husband is a super-capable, intelligent, responsible man, and I believed he had things under control. I read my book. I enjoyed listening to the children play. I kept them from bothering their daddy while he worked. I gave them some Oreos. Before long, the battery was replaced, my husband was my hero, I thanked him for taking care of the problem, and we had a wonderful evening at the beach!

This situation could have ended very differently. I could have disrespected my husband and tried to take over. I could have made demands or given him orders. I could have fumed or pouted. I could have gotten really angry and created a lot of tension between us and ruined our entire trip if I wanted to. When God's Spirit is in control of my heart, God can use things for my good and show me His provision and even miracles. I would have missed out seeing God send us an "angel" if I had mishandled this situation. I would have missed out on emotional intimacy with my husband and I would have set a poor example for our children about marriage or could have caused them to disrespect their dad. I could have spoiled our vacation. That is how much power I have with my choices and attitudes. God has ways of bringing people and circumstances into our lives that we can't predict when we are obeying Him and living by faith. Miracles are often waiting for us when we trust Him.

> "When God's Spirit is in control
> of my heart, God can use things
> for my good and show me His
> provision and even miracles."

My Story Blessed Another Wife

I posted the above story on my blog, then heard from this precious wife two days later:

> April,
>
> I don't really believe in coincidence, so I'm not sure what else to call this. . . . After I got done reading [this post], I thought to myself how this would be so hard for me to do if I were in your situation. I prayed for God to put a new heart in me and help me to be able to do this on a daily basis.

I guess God really heard me because He did just that! The next morning my husband and I started getting ready to head back home from visiting friends for Christmas. On our way home, we were low on gas. . . . We took the very first exit to get some gas, but [we were driving on fumes and the car didn't make it to the gas station.] What a nightmare! It was freezing outside. We had our 9-month-old with us and we hadn't eaten that morning. To top it off we were too far from home and too far from our friends. I started panicking but I didn't say anything (surprisingly) to make the situation worse—even though I felt like my husband should've taken care of this issue long ago!

I was reminded of your post . . . and I started shaking. I couldn't believe this was happening. I had prayed for a patient and submissive heart and now God put me in a situation that would test my character and grow me into a submissive wife. So I bit my tongue and listened to the Holy Spirit. As my husband stepped outside to figure what he could do, I held my daughter, prayed, sang worship songs, and read my Bible. Suddenly, I had this unexplainable peace come over me. I didn't fuss with my husband about how he should've listened to me. I simply followed his lead and allowed God to use him to be the leader [God] called him to be. I listened to his plan and suggestions. I tried comforting him by assuring him that the baby and I were okay and that everything would work out. God came through after eight hours! I was grateful for that time spent without things going my way. My husband was shocked! On our way home he told me how much my attitude meant to him. He praised God for what he saw in me that day—that gentle and quiet-spirited woman who is pleasing in the eyes of the Lord and her husband! The ride home was so sweet! My husband and I were on good terms without us fighting or being mad!

I don't know if you realize this, my precious sisters in Christ, but what happened that day when this couple ran out of gas is going to be something this particular husband *never* forgets. This is not at all the way this young wife normally would have reacted. I believe it will be a huge turning point in their marriage and a source of deeper intimacy, faith, and trust on both sides. I can't begin to tell you how grateful a husband in a situation like this would be for receiving grace instead of ridicule. This husband is likely going to be more motivated than ever to want to be the man God desires him to be and to take the best possible care of his precious wife because of his wife's godly response in the crisis they had on the side of the road.

Respecting Our Husbands During Conflict

Conflict will happen, yet God commands us to respond without sin even during disagreements. God desires all of us to avoid contention and complaining. We also never have a free pass to hold onto bitterness or unforgiveness in God's eyes. How can we approach conflict with our husbands in a way that honors them and honors Christ? Sometimes our husbands are wrong. They are human, after all. What about the fact that not every issue in marriage is resolvable? There will be some things about which we will just have to agree to disagree, give grace, and accept. There are some issues we may need to press them about a little more. Then there are some things against which we must take a firm stand, such as a husband's major unrepentant sin against us or our children, plans to lead us into sin, requests for us to condone sin, abuse directed toward ourselves or our children, something that is truly dangerous, or something that is very foolish. Sometimes it is critical for us to share our perspectives and ideas. Sometimes we must swiftly act. Other times, the best thing a wife can do is say nothing, pray, and wait on God to fight for her.

This topic humbles me greatly, because I am well aware that I don't personally have all of the answers. We all need the wisdom that only the Holy Spirit and God's Word can offer. I would, however, like to share a general framework for respecting our husbands during times of disappointment and conflict that will direct us all, myself included, to Christ and His Word. It is during these most trying times that we have the greatest opportunity to grow in our faith, to mature spiritually, and to watch God work on our behalf. Marital conflict is a place where God may powerfully use us to draw our husbands to Himself as we trust and obey Him. When a husband sees his wife respond with godliness and continue to honor his leadership when she strongly disagrees with him, *that* will get a man's full attention and pique his curiosity about her faith and her Lord.

> "When a husband sees his wife respond with godliness and continue to honor his leadership when she strongly disagrees with him, *that* will get a man's full attention and pique his curiosity about her faith and her Lord."

BEFORE YOU ADDRESS THE CONFLICT

1. Apply Scripture to conflict.

This is always the best place to start! There are many verses in Scripture about handling conflict in godly ways. An idea for personal Bible study would be to use a concordance or a website to look up all the words you can find that have to do with conflict and read those passages. I would suggest looking up key words: anger, argue, bitterness, conflict, contentious, division, divorce, fight, forgive, peace, quarrels, and temper. There are also websites where you can look up topics such as, "What does the Bible say about conflict?"

Here are some verses to get us in the right frame of mind for discussing how to handle conflict in a way that honors God:

Do not conform to the pattern of this world, but be transformed by the renewing of your mind. Then you will be able to test and approve what God's will is—his good, pleasing and perfect will. (Rom. 12:2)

If you harbor bitter envy and selfish ambition in your hearts, do not boast about it or deny the truth. Such "wisdom" does not come down from heaven but is earthly, unspiritual, demonic. For where you have envy and selfish ambition, there you find disorder and every evil practice. But the wisdom that comes from heaven is first of all pure; then peace-loving, considerate, submissive, full of mercy and good fruit, impartial and sincere. Peacemakers who sow in peace reap a harvest of righteousness. (James 3:14–18)

For our struggle is not against flesh and blood, but against the rulers, against the authorities, against the powers of this dark world and against the spiritual forces of evil in the heavenly realms. (Eph. 6:12)

The weapons we fight with are not the weapons of the world. On the contrary, they have divine power to demolish strongholds. We demolish arguments and every pretension that sets itself up against the knowledge of God, and we take captive every thought to make it obedient to Christ. (2 Cor. 10:4–5)

Do not repay anyone evil for evil. Be careful to do what is right in the eyes of everyone. If it is possible, as far as it depends on you, live at peace with everyone. Do not take revenge, my dear friends, but leave room for God's wrath, for it is written: "It is mine to avenge; I will repay," says the Lord. On the contrary: "If your enemy is hungry, feed him; if he is thirsty, give him something to drink. In doing this, you will heap burning coals on his head." Do not be overcome by evil, but overcome evil with good. (Rom. 12:17–21)

> *Lord,*
>
> *I acknowledge my total dependence on You in every area of my life. I renounce my worldly wisdom. I ask You to reveal any wrong motives in my heart when I approach conflict and disappointment. You have not given me a spirit of fear, but a spirit of power and love, and a sound mind. Open my eyes to all of the enemy's tactics. You can give me the power to disagree with my husband without arguing or sinning. You alone can give me the wisdom I need about exactly how to approach my husband in any conflict. Let me not fear conflict, but help me to see that it is a pathway through which You will demonstrate Your power and glory to me and to my husband.*
>
> *In the name and power of Christ, amen!*

2. Remember that your husband is not the enemy.

In the heat of conflict, it is easy to feel like your husband is your enemy. But the Bible says that "our struggle is not against flesh and blood" (Eph. 6:12). My husband is not my enemy; Satan is my real enemy. It is important for me to acknowledge who my real enemy is and what he desires for me. He has plans to steal, kill, and destroy in my spiritual life, my marriage, and every part of my life. If I can refuse to look at my husband as my enemy, but see him as my teammate and brother (or potential future brother) in Christ, God will empower me to see him with His holy eyes. If I can remember that many times the real issue is just that my husband and I think differently and perceive the world differently because we are unique people with vastly different backgrounds and filters through which we perceive reality then I can move toward him with patience and a desire to know his heart without judging him harshly. I can refuse to assume evil motives on my husband's part and leave room for the possibility that he sees things in ways I have never even imagined before.

> "My husband is not my enemy;
> Satan is my real enemy."

3. Seek to understand his perspective before sharing yours.

So many times conflict arises when one person does not feel "heard" or understood. It has been my experience that a large number of the conflicts between husbands and wives escalate unnecessarily because one or both spouses do not feel validated in their perspective. We may not be able to guarantee that we feel heard by our husbands, but we can seek to be sure our husbands feel that we are listening and that we want to understand. I can communicate that I value his ideas and that I am open and receptive toward anything he wants to share with me, even if I don't agree with my husband. If he states an opinion about something to me that makes me bristle and with which I feel I cannot agree, instead of immediately telling him I can't agree with him or labeling him as "wrong," I can listen and ask friendly, curious questions. I might say things like:

- That is an interesting perspective that I have never considered before. Would you mind telling me more about your thoughts on this?
- Do I understand correctly that you think X? I'd love to hear more about your thought processes on this issue.
- That is a totally new way of looking at this issue for me. Would you mind sharing a bit more about how you began to think this way?

When my husband shares more, I want to try to be in a receptive mind-set with the primary goal of trying to get inside my husband's world and his perspective to get to know him better. I am not asking questions as an interrogation or as an attorney who is cross-examining a witness trying to build my case. I am simply seeking to better understand. It is entirely possible that I might learn something I never knew about my husband and that I might better connect with his heart and his legitimate concerns if I am willing to stop and listen. I might realize that we don't actually disagree, but that we have different priorities that are both good. Or I may realize that my husband and I do disagree but I will be able to sympathize with the valid points of his position. Even if I don't agree with my husband, I can look for the things that are true in his perspective and validate those things.

After my husband has presented everything he desires to share, then I might summarize back to him what he said so that he knows I understand him well. Then if I believe it is appropriate, I may decide to share my perspective in a friendly way.

- You make such a great point about X. I really appreciate your explanation about your perspective on this. I feel like I got to know you a little better because of what you shared with me. If this would be a good time, I'd love to share the way I look at this issue.
- You know, I think I would like to take some time to pray about this issue before I share my thoughts with you. I'd really like to think about your ideas for a day or two.

Shaunti Feldhahn's book *For Women Only*[1] taught me to realize that most of the time when I was upset with Greg and thought he was being unloving, the real issue was a simple misunderstanding. I have seen this with so many other wives, as well. With enough practice and accurate information from men in general and from your husband in particular, you can learn to understand your husband's perspectives instead of assuming that your husband has evil motives toward you when you feel unloved. Most of the time a husband really doesn't want to hurt his wife. I know there are some rare exceptions, but most husbands are not secretly planning how they can make their wife feel miserable or unloved. Often what seems like an unloving response (from a wife's perspective) is really the husband reacting to feeling disrespected or misunderstood. Or it may be that wives just think so very differently that we cannot begin to predict what our husbands are thinking until we hear more information. The worst thing a wife can do, in my view, is to assume that her husband thinks exactly like she does, and if he is doing something that upsets her, he must have intentionally tried to upset her. A wife fares best when she does not assume that she understands her husband's perspectives, but waits before judging him. There can be much wisdom in choosing to assume the best about our husbands—that there must be some explanation we just don't understand quite yet.

4. Prayerfully determine if you need to speak about the issue.

As a wife, I have a responsibility to know my ideas, feelings, and concerns about decisions—particularly important decisions—and to share them with my husband respectfully. I am to be a trusted advisor to my husband and his dearest, most respected friend. It is terribly wrong for me to say nothing if I see my husband heading in a dangerous, unwise, or sinful direction (for biblical examples, see the story of Abigail in 1 Samuel 25, and of Sapphira in Acts 5:1–11). God will hold me accountable for failing to use my influence if I see a major problem and I don't address it.

God uses husbands to speak to wives. And God uses wives to speak to husbands, too, as we are abiding in Him and are not being controlled by the flesh. Biblical submission is not about mindless obedience or slave-like subservience. It is not about making our husbands decide everything for us as if they were our fathers. God desires us to be women who have our own personhood, faith, and ideas. God's design for submission is that we as wives submit from a position of great strength and power in Christ, with intelligence and meekness (bridled strength), and that we are prepared for times when we must firmly stand for what is right and even confront sin when necessary. Ultimately, our calling is to please, honor, and obey Christ. We long to please both Jesus and our husbands, but if we must choose between the two, we must choose Jesus.

> "We long to please both Jesus and our husbands, but if we must choose between the two, we must choose Jesus."

Here is something amazing about living for Christ Jesus—He is totally sovereign. He can change my circumstances at any time, in any way. He can do miracles. He can change my heart. He can change my husband's heart. If my husband makes a decision with which I don't agree, I can pray and seek God's will about that decision, and God can change my husband's mind much more effectively than I ever could. God can convict my husband of sin and open his eyes to His truth in ways I never could. The great difficulty is, how do we determine when to speak up, and when to simply wait on God and allow Him to do the work? Again, this will require incredible sensitivity on the part of each wife to the Spirit's still, small voice and gentle nudging.

I would really love for there to be some formula that we can always go to and follow a series of steps and then the conflict is solved, but God doesn't generally work that way. He requires us to walk by faith without knowing how to solve the problems, trusting Him for the light we need for just the next step. Only God knows what we ought to do in each circumstance. We will need to be very careful about seeking outside advice during times of conflict, because there are many sources of counsel who will steer us in unbiblical directions that will damage our marriages further. We must weigh everything anyone says against Scripture before following that person's advice. I believe we will each need to stay in constant prayer, repenting of any sin in our own lives daily, praising God, having grateful hearts, being filled with the Holy Spirit, and seeking God above all else, depending completely on Him for wisdom and direction in order to approach conflict constructively.

WHEN YOU BELIEVE GOD DESIRES THAT YOU ADDRESS SOMETHING

There are some general scriptural principles of handling conflict that we will consider. You may also want to take time to bathe these kinds of issues in much prayer, possibly even with fasting, until you have a very solid sense of what God is directing you to do, just like Esther did before she approached her husband, the king, about a potentially deadly conflict (Esther 4:12–16).

Some ideas to prayerfully consider:

1. Be gentle in your tone of voice and demeanor (Prov. 15:1).
2. Do not bring up old issues from the past that have been forgiven (1 Cor. 13:5).
3. Be quick to listen, slow to speak, and slow to become angry (James 1:19).
4. Listen to his concerns, wisdom, ideas, and opinions carefully, and give him your undivided attention (James 1:19).
5. Care about what he is saying and hear his heart (1 Cor. 13:4–5).
6. Look beyond any anger to see the pain behind it and see how God might desire you to attempt to make things right between you and your husband (Matt. 5:24).
7. Ask questions to clarify if you can't seem to agree with your husband: "Honey, I think I understand you to mean this. Am I hearing you correctly?" (Phil. 2:4).
8. Pray for God to give your husband His wisdom and for His will

to be done, as you thank God for your husband and his leadership and protection in your life (Matt. 6:10; 1 Thess. 5:18).

9. Hold the outcome of every decision loosely in your hands, allowing God to work His will in each situation. Place God's desires
far above your own, whatever His will might be; this is how you
take up your cross and follow Christ (Luke 9:23).

10. Realize that God can and will speak to you through your husband.
Listen carefully and thoughtfully to any constructive criticism,
ideas, suggestions, or rebukes he may have. Don't defend yourself.
Prayerfully consider what your husband said and ask God to help
you see if these are things you need to change or whether that
particular criticism is something to let go. A wise woman humbly
heeds a rebuke and embraces correction, knowing that is how she
learns and becomes more wise (Prov. 15:12, 32).

Confronting A Husband About His Sin

We can seek to address our husbands in a God-honoring way when
we believe they are wrong. That is what we need from them, as well. All
of us, as believers, are to speak the truth in love to others. It is not a gift
to ignore a brother's or sister's sin. We must be careful to balance truth
and love carefully. Too much truth and not enough love, and we will
come across as being harsh and judgmental. Too much love and not
enough truth, and we will not be effective at confronting sin properly. I
pray that we will have the power of Christ to extend grace, mercy, and
forgiveness to our husbands, just as we so desperately need these things
ourselves at times.

Sometimes we will only pray. Other times, we do need to speak
against our husbands' sin as the Spirit directs us. It is important for us
to keep in mind that if a husband is an unbeliever, his greatest need is
Christ, and he may not be able to have victory and power over sin because he needs the Spirit of God and salvation. You can address his sin,
but, ultimately, until God opens his eyes and convicts him and brings

him to life spiritually, he is spiritually dead. If there is only one believer in Christ in the marriage, the responsibility rests on that person's shoulders completely to set the godly example.

Here are some suggestions to prayerfully consider when deciding if you must confront your husband:

- You must repent of your own sin and have your own life straight with God and your husband. You can't see your husband's sin clearly when you're caught up in your own sin (Matt. 7:1–5). We have no credibility with our men if we confront them and they can see unrepentant sin in our lives.
- You must restore your husband gently, being careful not to fall into temptation to sin yourself (perhaps with unforgiveness, resentment, or bitterness), as Scripture warns (Gal. 6:1).
- You must be sure you don't have sinful motives. Our only motives must be to love God with all our hearts, minds, souls, and strength, and to love our husbands with the love of Christ (Matt. 22:37–39).
- You can share your heart and your pain privately with your husband (Matt. 18:15). You should try to choose a good time when your husband is best able to hear you if possible, such as when he is well-rested, fed, not overly stressed, and in a decent mood.
- You will need sensitivity to God's Spirit to know exactly what to say, how to say it, and when to say it versus when silence is the best approach. If we are being led by the Spirit, love, joy, and peace will result; if we are not being led by the Spirit, we'll be conceited, envying others, provoking them, and causing division (Gal. 5:16–26).
- You cannot force your husband to do what you want. You can share your heart briefly and vulnerably, with gentleness, kindness, and respect. Then you must wait on God to bring conviction and allow your husband to choose repentance (John 16:7–11).
- You are responsible for your own obedience to God and you may

not follow your husband into sin. You don't have to participate in sin even if your husband decides to. You can make it clear in a firm yet polite way what your limits and boundaries are. If your husband is a believer, you can show him relevant Bible verses to back up your stance. Your covenant with Christ far surpasses your covenant with your husband (Acts 5:29).

- You may need to create boundaries or consequences if your husband refuses to repent. Your exact course of action would vary depending on the issue and God's prompting. But there are times when a husband continues in infidelity, criminal activity, drug or alcohol addiction, or abuse, when a wife needs to separate from him until he is receiving the outside help he needs and proves over a significant period of time that he has changed and he is willing to rebuild trust (1 Cor. 7:10–16).

If You Can't Arrive at an Agreement

The primary reason I should submit to my husband's leadership even when I disagree is that God commands wives to submit to their husbands in everything *as to the Lord* (which means, unless my husband asks me to sin or condone sin, or he is not in his right mind). If I belong to Christ and He is my Lord, I reverence Him and submit to Him in everything. God is concerned with our motives and faithfulness, even when we don't agree with what He asked us to do and even if the issue seems small to us. If God gives us an assignment or command, it is important to Him that we obey.

Whoever can be trusted with very little can also be trusted with much, and whoever is dishonest with very little will also be dishonest with much. (Luke 16:10)

Our willingness to fully submit to God, even when we don't understand or agree with Him, brings Him joy and allows us to abide close to Him, which brings us joy. Our obedience also accomplishes glory for Christ and for the gospel. Our willingness to cooperate with our husbands even when we disagree also shows our husbands that we trust them and that we trust God to lead us through them. A wife's trust and willingness to follow her husband even when she disagrees tends to inspire her husband to step up and become more responsible. When a husband feels the weight of the whole decision on his shoulders, it motivates him like nothing else can to really try to make the best and most selfless decision for his family. He doesn't want to let his wife and family down. He wants to be the hero! It's funny how when a wife approaches things as God instructs her to, God often works in mysterious ways. The husband's mind sometimes changes. The wife's mind sometimes changes. Circumstances change. Miracles happen. Sometimes God had something much better in mind than the wife or husband could ever have imagined, even if things were hard for a while. God strengthens our faith in Him through these experiences.

There may be times when a wife feels that her husband's decision was wrong and she may still believe it was wrong years later as she looks back. In those times, a wife can still trust God to be at work fulfilling Romans 8:28–29. Perhaps God will use that wrong decision to teach her husband about being a better leader. Maybe God will use a husband's failure or wrong choice to teach a wife about faith, the sufficiency of Christ, the power of prayer, and the sovereignty of God. God is a master at taking a big mess and turning it into something beautiful. A husband will make mistakes. Sometimes he will fail. How a wife handles such a situation can either inspire a husband to want to become more like Christ or can cause him to feel paralyzed, discouraged, and depressed. In these critical moments, you have the opportunity to be your husband's greatest supporter, fan, and cheerleader, and you have the opportunity to allow your godly character to shine as the Spirit empowers you. You could most easily crush your husband's spirit if you are not careful in your responses. When we obey God, our time is never wasted and our efforts are never futile. He sees our obedience and He promises to reward us for our faithfulness when we stand before Him in heaven.

> "God is a master at taking a
> big mess and turning it into
> something beautiful."

Whoever sows to please their flesh, from the flesh will reap destruction; whoever sows to please the Spirit, from the Spirit will reap eternal life. Let us not become weary in doing good, for at the proper time we will reap a harvest if we do not give up. (Gal. 6:8–9)

"Look, I am coming soon! My reward is with me, and I will give to each person according to what they have done." (Rev. 22:12)

RECOGNIZING AN APOLOGY

Many times we expect our husbands to apologize verbally when they have wronged us. But some people apologize without words. It makes sense that if a particular man solves problems without words, processes emotions without words, and maybe prays without words, that he might also apologize without words. Some men of action believe that a verbal apology is meaningless. If he brings you a gift (either something tangible or an offer to do something for you or with you) or comes to you after a disagreement wanting to have sex with you, he may be trying to apologize in his own way. If you are able to recognize his intentions, you might verbalize what you believe he is saying and see how he responds: "This is so sweet of you to reach out to me like this. That takes a lot of courage and shows me that you really do love me very much. Thank you for leading the way to restore peace." If he shows that he is, in fact, apologizing in his own way, you could smile and hug him and receive his offer and say, "Apology accepted." Or, you could share what you need to feel closure. "Your gesture is so thoughtful. You make me feel very loved. I am so verbal, it would mean a lot to me if you might also use some words along with your sweet gift. Then I know my heart will feel totally at peace." Or you might apologize with words first if you need to, and maybe you can also offer your own tangible gift as well.

HANDLING DISAPPOINTMENTS

Imagine that you and your husband cannot agree about a decision. You have shared your convictions, your preferences, your concerns, your thoughts, and feelings with your husband respectfully yet he strongly believes that God desires him to buy a car that is more expensive than what you would prefer.

- Acknowledge your disappointment and your concerns to God.
- Pray and ask God for His will and His glory, not your will, to be done, following Jesus's example of submission in Luke 22:42.
- Thank God and thank your husband for any godly leadership he exercises.
- Focus on all the wonderful things there are about this situation for which you can choose to be grateful, and on God's vision for His glory in this body of His beloved followers (Phil. 4:8).
- Wait on God, give Him the desires of your heart, and trust Him to do what is best for you, your husband, and your family that He might accomplish His purposes and His will (Rom. 8:28–29).
- Love the Lord your God with all your heart, with all your soul, with all your strength, and with all your mind (Luke 10:27).
- Remember that our heart attitude and our obedience to God as wives are more important than whether we get to do things our way in various circumstances.

- Ask God to work powerfully in your husband's heart, mind, and soul to bless him, build him up, and help him to grow in spiritual maturity.
- Recognize that God may be leading your husband and family in this direction for reasons that are beyond your understanding at this point in time. Joyfully anticipate God's perfect will and His plan unfolding for your family here as a result of your husband's leadership.

If Your Husband Is Not a Believer

If your husband is not yet a believer, he probably can't hear any of your words about God right now, but he will notice your respect, joy, peace, and quiet faith in Jesus. In addition to the commands that apply to all believers and all wives, God's assignment for you, until your husband does receive Christ, is 1 Peter 3:1–6. (See the appendix: Reaching a Husband Who Doesn't Know Christ.) Thank your husband if he allows you to go to church. Be sure he knows he is welcome to come anytime, but don't try to force him to go with you.

If he doesn't want you to go to church, share your desire to go and ask if there is a different church or different schedule that would be better for him. But if he insists that he does not want you to go, consider honoring his leadership as you fervently pray for God to intervene in the situation to allow you to go to church again (or to at least be able to be involved in a women's Bible study during the week or an online Christian women's group). You might say, "Baby, I really want to be able to go to church every Sunday. I want our children to go to church, too. It is very important to me. I will be so sad if I can't go. But if you believe this is best for our family, I will trust your leadership." I have seen this approach soften the hearts of many unbelieving husbands to God and to their wives, even though I realize it would be completely counterintuitive and it would be painful. If a husband comes to Christ because of a wife's willingness to honor his leadership even in this issue, I believe it would be completely worth that sacrifice of not going to church temporarily. Whatever will draw him to God and whatever God prompts the wife to do is more important than a wife's preferences at the time.

There are also times when God clearly reveals to a wife that she should go to church with her children even if her husband doesn't want her to go. This requires a woman to be very sensitive to God's prompting. But there can be times when a wife might say, "Honey, I want to honor you as the head of our home, but I know that God wants me and our children in church. I don't want to be negligent toward you. But this is something I believe I must do. Is there a particular church or schedule that would work best? I want to honor you and God."

> "A cooperative wife draws a husband to God much more easily than a contentious wife ever could."

A cooperative wife draws a husband to God much more easily than a contentious wife ever could. Continue seeking God with all your heart privately, ask God to help you grow spiritually, stay in the Bible, listen to online solid biblical teaching, pursue friendship with some godly wives, and teach your children about God at home, reading the Bible and praying with them in a way that honors your husband and God. It may be that you do this for a time and then God may speak to your heart to return to church with your children. Go to church with your children if you know that God desires you to approach the situation this way. Do what you believe in your heart and mind that God is calling you to do as you seek to obey and please Him far above anything else.

Some Husbands' Thoughts on Conflict

Husband 1

When a wife argues with her husband constantly about small things and insists on her way without taking his ideas . . . into account, it quickly creates an environment where the husband can start to believe that he does not have much value in his wife's life or their marriage.

Husband 2

To me, it's a sign of respect when someone who doesn't agree with me tells why he/she doesn't agree instead of disagreeing in silence. As a leader of any kind, you should solicit input from others, especially from people who have a different perspective—and men and women usually have different perspectives.

Husband 3

Respect that (his) decision . . . has its own merits, even if it is different than how you would do it. Don't invalidate your husband's choice. Is God working through your husband at this particular time in a way that you cannot see? Examine if you disagree based upon biblical principle. If it is sin, then you have a right to quote Scripture and voice that you may not agree with that course of action. *One time.* Don't repeat yourself over and over. We get it. We have heard you. We may still disagree but we cannot refute biblical principles and the Holy Spirit will speak to us. . . .

Say something like, "I want to bring this to your attention. There is an observation I've made that makes me feel uncomfortable. When is a good time to talk about it?" . . . If he doesn't get back to you, gently ask him in a reasonable amount of time for a follow up. If he still doesn't get back to you and the sin needs to be addressed, then follow Matthew 18:15–17 on conflict resolution. Pick your battles. If the sin is something that God can work out with your husband, He will. If it's something really important that is affecting your husband's walk and it is something that needs to be addressed, then do pursue it. . . . Be prepared to ask someone he is confident with to help you out, but give him time to address the issue with you. Never go above his head without trying a few times first.

Husband 4

I expect my wife to disagree with me. I want my wife to disagree with me. . . . [O]nly a fool thinks he's never mistaken or wrong. . . . I value and trust her opinion and I would hope she would respect me enough to save me from myself when necessary. "Respect" doesn't mean "timid" (2 Tim. 1:7).

Husband 5

I would not want a mindless doormat for a wife. I want a wife who has a brain, and who will share her thoughts, advice, and counsel with me. If I'm about to do something stupid, I want to know about it. And if I'm about to do something stupid that will hurt my family, I especially want to know about it. But what I don't want is for her to try to force me to do things her way. . . . If your actions and attitude inspire trust in your husband, then you will have credibility when you disagree with him. But if you are always competing with him or doing other things that cause him not to trust you, then . . . when you disagree with him, he will think you have an ulterior motive. Be specific about the things you are concerned about, but tell him in a gentle, soft, non-threatening way. You will be much more likely to get results using that approach, as opposed to approaching him in a harsh, accusing manner. Keep in mind that the point here is restoration, not punishment. . . . In the case of sin, you are speaking to him as his sister in Christ and as his friend.

Conflict is a tough topic for all of us. It may be scary to think about your husband being angry with you. Thankfully, God's perfect love can cast out our fear, even our fear of conflict. Or you may struggle with pride and self-reliance and have difficulty accepting someone else's decisions as valid. Disagreements, disappointments, and failures present powerful opportunities for us to learn to approach our husbands in God's wisdom so that our marriages are actually strengthened during disagreements. Each conflict is a stage upon which we have the chance to demonstrate the power of God at work in our lives. Each disagreement can be a gateway through which we see God work miracles and answer prayers in ways beyond our ability to fathom. Conflicts in our marriages can become blessings and bridges to greater intimacy with God and our husbands when we approach them in God's strength, love, power, and wisdom.

Sharing the Journey

Sometimes it helps for us to hear the perspectives and voices of other people who are learning the same things we want to learn. Each person has a unique way of explaining and sharing that helps us expand our own understanding. I know that I've been blessed by the insights and stories of my Peaceful Wife's blog readers, and they've graciously agreed to allow their words to be included here. I pray that their stories might impact and inspire you for God's glory in your life!

FROM PEACEFUL WIFE'S BLOG READERS

Erin's Story

My husband and I were separated and on the road to divorce a few years ago. We came back together and sought much counseling and healing. . . . I saw that, honestly, I had been raised to show men disrespect. Once we had children, my husband became like a child to me; I disciplined him, came down on him, and nagged him like he was five years old. I had lots of pride and ideas about what I thought was right and how we should run our household. His opinion didn't really matter to me and I would fight for my way to the death. One of the most monumental things I read [on your blog] in the beginning is that he is not only an adult but that he has the right to his own opinions and choices. There is nothing that says he should do things the way I think we should do them. Quite frankly, how would I feel if he condemned everything I did? What a horrible way to live. The very first change I made was just to respect him as an adult. . . . My husband is a very active father and, with the surprise of our last child, God has given us both a new opportunity to do parenthood "the right way." He never felt like he could be a parent before. There was no room for him to do anything with the kids. I made all the decisions. I always took the children's sides. I kept him on the outside. He felt unwelcomed and felt like . . . I really wanted to be a single mom. I never allowed space for him to even try. Now I invite him into most decisions. If the kids ask questions about things they can do, my default is, "We will have to talk to Daddy." He keeps the children on his own more—I trust he can handle them and he is very capable now. . . . One of the biggest changes I had to make was realizing that when I would pitch a fit if things didn't go my way, it made me look like a spoiled, little, bratty child. My habits have changed, and though I am far from perfect, I know my husband feels respected. I smile more. I compliment him more. I realize my happiness is important to him and he doesn't do things to try to make me unhappy. I realized how many horrible thoughts I had about my husband's motives that were so far from true.

An Interview with Bryan

April: It's typical for a woman to believe that if she respects her husband, her husband's ego will be built up too much and that he will become prideful. What would you say to that?

Bryan: I would tell her to first seek God and His wisdom. If she isn't right with God, nothing good will come from her trying to submit and respect. She will harbor resentment each time she tries and fails to show respect. The same goes for the husband, but we'll stick with her.

All things are possible through God. Without seeking to follow His designs, you will surely fail. The Bible clearly says that it is the duty of a wife to respect and biblically submit to her husband, and tells her that if her husband isn't a Christian, that he may be won over by her behavior and respect. . . . If he takes the submission thing too far and treats her poorly, then he needs to seek God and His rules for male headship. If he is an abusive man who simply cannot change, then she needs to seek godly, experienced help, and may need to separate from him, at least for a time. There is a big problem these days with women and biblical submission/respect. They listen to their friends about marriage instead of listening to God. When most women don't behave properly, why would you go to them for wisdom? Turn to God; He never fails!

April: When your wife began to show real trust, respect, honor, and faith in you, how did that make you feel about her? How did that motivate you in the marriage? How did you want to respond to her?

Bryan: I'm going to be frank in this part a bit. In all honesty, when we were at the tipping point of our marriage, it was "fix it or be done." There wasn't much romance, sex, laughter, talking, sharing, or anything. We were fighting almost every day and just miserable. I finally broke down and turned to God to help me. I opened my Bible, prayed, researched marriage, surfed the web for ideas and similar situations, and eventually compiled a solution. I went to my wife and simply told her this is what has to happen or we will never make it—that God has a very specific plan that needs to be followed. I also told her that it's a two-way street, and we both have changing to do. Yes, it seems like the women have more to do when it comes to submission and respect, but men have one very large responsibility on top of their list of changes. That's answering to God. Men are to be the head of the family and are held accountable for everything when standing before God.

As we started on our journey it was rough. She really tried very hard to listen and follow the words in Scripture. As the days and weeks went by . . . I started to see a whole new woman, and she was beautiful! This new and improved woman was quiet, soft, respectful, and just (frankly) sexy to me! We became closer every day and the desires came back. Our sex life was like it was twenty years ago! As she changed herself, I felt better about myself and it showed through my actions toward her. . . . We are back into the church more often, we pray together every morning and evening, and our kids are even behaving better. I know it sounds strange, but the kids have seen the new us and they love it as well. Their grades have even improved. . . . She is a huge blessing to me and I couldn't imagine my life without her. All it takes is one simple thing: follow God's plan. It will get easier as time passes.

Angie's Story

I'm certainly not "there yet" with having all the answers, but becoming Christ-like is a process and a journey, not a destination. . . . I am productivity-driven and goal-oriented. My husband, who is extremely smart and has a mathematical mind that I admire, simply does not operate the same way and it was an immediate source of tension. I felt frustrated, unloved, and lonely. The worst part came, however, when my husband had an affair. . . . We separated. Our families rallied around to support our son and me, and tried hard (with no success) at reaching out to him. We headed quickly into divorce talks. My husband did not want anything to do with me. It was devastating, more than words can tell. In this sorrow, grief, despair, and hopelessness, I reached out to God to carry me through. I pleaded with Him to give me hope and to allow me a life after this kind of loss. I wore myself thin trying to "fix" the problems myself, trying to win my husband back or move along to a new life without him. It was in a particular prayer to the Lord that I got an answer. I remember being so numb and tired that I just listened. God clearly told me to stop "getting in the way," to stop worrying about what is happening, to trust Him with the situation, to be patient, to look up at Him and not at the world crumbling around me. I had exhausted all of my other options and efforts already, so I did what God told me to do. My husband and I reconciled, only through God's divine plan, I am completely sure. We have been abundantly blessed in our marriage since then and now have three children. My husband is a completely new man.

When I step out of my God-given place and try to take over or lead, I step *into* God's way of disciplining His child and making it right. God loves our children and me as much as He loves my husband. I do not serve only my husband; I serve God, too. Now I allow the failures and successes my husband has without stepping into God's path of rebuke or blessings. When I pray during particularly hard times, I pray for steadfastness for myself, for patience, and a calm spirit (I am the one who likes to pick fights). I pray for my husband to have wisdom, courage, and selflessness. Our marriage is stronger, more resilient, and flourishes now. My gentle spirit has allowed my husband to step into his role as an excellent provider, husband, and father.

Veronica's Story

I . . . have been married to my loving husband, Dong, for nine years. . . . He is my best friend. Having had no godly role models in marriage, I went into marriage not really knowing what my role was as a wife. So . . . I suggested ways of making him improve himself, researched job openings and forced him to apply, and constantly told him to pursue his passions. While he was undecided on his life, I decided to lead our family while waiting for him to get his act together. My "wearing the pants" in the relationship made me feel very unfeminine, depressed, bitter, and resentful of him and his perceived faults.

After the birth of our fourth child, I suddenly felt the urge to just stay home and take care of our children. I was tired of leading. I gave up my desire to control my husband on September 1, 2013. I also decided to submit to God around that time, too. . . . I never knew that a passive husband would never lead when led by a dominant wife! That was me!

I was an overachieving, Type A control freak who was perfectionistic and driven. I didn't know that my super-efficiency was getting in the way of my husband's leadership. The Lord opened my eyes to my sins: that I was prideful, judgmental, self-righteous, and (though I would never have verbalized it) had not much faith in God but lots of faith in myself. I repented and was appalled at the level of my wrongdoings! I couldn't speak for days. I was scared to open up my mouth, lest I further disrespect my husband.

Since I have been biblically submissive, I have been experiencing a kind of joy that is hard to explain. You've got to experience it to believe it! Freedom from the bondage of control has given me so much peace. . . . Now, I wouldn't go back to my former controlling self for anything. . . .

My learning to respect my husband has given our home so much joy, peace, and love. Dong was so pleased with my transformation that he even asked me to blog about my journey a few short weeks after I submitted to him! He said that he wanted more couples to experience what we were experiencing and to discover the joy that can be found within marriage! This coming from a man whom I have largely disrespected and almost emasculated due to my cluelessness! Ever since I submitted to God and to my husband, Dong has been stepping up to the plate. He has dreams and plans now—and though things are just starting to fall into place—I see a bright future ahead. When I shut up, that's when Dong started hearing God's voice. When I stopped deciding, that's when he started leading. When I started focusing on my own role in the family, that's when he started blooming into the man God wanted him to be!

All these years, my prayers were geared toward God changing him! Only when I changed my prayers to "Lord, search *my* heart and change how I view things" did God start to hear my prayers. . . . My honoring my husband's leadership has seeped through other areas of our lives as well. I decided to let go of my overly busy broadcasting career to take on the role of helpmeet for Dong. I want to be there for him and support him 100 percent in his business endeavors while also taking care of our four little ones. Before, my husband would be too lazy to go to church; now it is he who sometimes initiates going. Before, our kids were confused as to who was "boss" in the house. . . . Now they know that Daddy has the last say in all things. . . . Among friends and extended family, I make sure they know that I now do not make any important decision without first consulting with my husband. I am lucky that my husband has always found me desirable, and now that I am submissive, even more so. What changed was how I now give of myself totally in the marriage act whereas before it felt like a chore. Being a peaceful wife has blessed me in all areas of my life. I couldn't thank God enough for changing my heart and giving me His peace, the peace that the world cannot give.

Alana's Tips

If I could go back and talk to myself at the beginning of this journey to become a wife that does marriage God's way, there are several things I would say to myself to (hopefully) make this process simpler and easier than it has been.

1. R-E-L-A-X! It is really okay if you don't get all of this today, tomorrow, or the next day. Breathe! Take your time! Be patient with yourself.
2. Focus on only one or two things at a time. You have all of your life to do this. There is no time limit. This is not something that you learn once and you are done. Think of it as a continuing education program. If you try to do it all right now, you will get overwhelmed. Slow down and just work on one or two things at a time. When those become comfortable, you can add in one or two more. Do not pressure yourself!
3. It will feel awkward. Nothing about this is going to feel normal to you. Accept that. In time, it will become normal to you.

4. The things your husband needs from you are very different than the things you need from him. Some of them seem like they are so little and inconsequential but they really do matter to him even if they would mean very little to you. That is because you are different and have different needs. Just trust that these things do matter to him even if you don't understand it.

5. Men are very different creatures than women. It is almost un-imaginable how different we are. God created us differently for a purpose. Don't assume you understand what he is thinking and why he is acting the way that he is. If you are unsure why he is doing what he is doing, ask. If you have the right attitude, he will probably be more than happy to explain.

6. Listen to him. Really listen. The truth is that he is probably will-ing to talk to you and share his heart if you are willing to listen. He means what he says. Believe him. Don't be so busy formu-lating your words back to him that you miss the message in his words. He is giving you some great information to understand him and your relationship if you will just listen.

7. Be a student of men in general, and your husband in particu-lar. Men operate in their own unique world that you [may] know nothing about. You probably don't understand how they think, what they mean, or how they feel. There are ways you can learn about this, though. You can read, study, and learn. Most of all, see #6!

8. God knows what works in marriage. He *created* marriage. He knows it better than anyone else. Therefore, it is going to work best only when we follow His plan. It may seem backward, out of style, or old-fashioned to be a biblically submissive and re-spectful wife, but it works. God says that we should "Stand at the crossroads and look; ask for the ancient paths, ask where the good way is, and walk in it, and you will find rest for your souls" (Jer. 6:16). This ancient path is certainly good, and you will find so much rest when you follow God's plan.

9. Rest in your husband's love for you. You have wasted so much time worrying over if he loves you, how much he loves you, and why he isn't showing it the way you wish. Just rest in his love for you (unless he blatantly says he doesn't love you, he is cheating on you, or he is actually abusing you). It is secure, and you have no need to worry.

10. You will get better at this. Don't be discouraged. It takes time. You will be a student of learning about doing marriage God's way for life, but with time, it will get easier and start feeling more comfortable. Just hang in there.

11. You must, must have time with God each day. Try your best to get this in. If for some reason you didn't get to have time with God that day, be especially on guard for your own wrong thinking and misbehavior!

12. Your husband does have feelings. It seems like he doesn't because he is big and strong, but behind that big tough exterior is a fragile heart.

13. Prayer journaling and writing is powerful. It gives you a chance to process what you are learning and thinking while growing closer to God in the process.

14. Pray, pray, pray! You cannot do this without God as your partner! Pray for help, wisdom, protection, and knowledge. Pray about specific little situations. Pray about the big things.

15. This is not really about your marriage. It is about *you* and your obedience to God. It is your job to focus on your walk with Him and let God focus on your husband. Even if you never see change, you need to be okay with that. Focus on what your responsibility is in this marriage. Focus on becoming a better Christian woman and wife.

16. Just keep going. You are going to mess up and fall. You are going to have days you want to throw in the towel. Don't expect perfection out of yourself. When you do mess up, forgive yourself, get back up, and keep going. Do not allow discouragement to defeat you.

FROM APRIL

And now, my precious sister in Christ, *your* story begins. I cannot wait to add all that God does in and through you and in your marriage to this collection of wives' miraculous stories. God doesn't promise to change our husbands as we obey Him, seek Him, love Him, and desire Him far above all else. He does promise to change *us!* If God is going to change our husbands for His glory, it will only be as we do things His way. Our motives are so key here. I cannot embark on this journey in order to change my husband and to make him love me the way I want him to. My goal has to be simply to love, obey, honor, and please Christ and to love, honor, and bless my husband. I trust God with the results and the timing of those results. I trust that He will use me for His greatest glory however He sees fit. I find all of my fulfillment, contentment, identity, value, joy, and peace in Christ alone. Then I can be unshakable no matter what happens in my life.

The thing I look forward to in heaven—after seeing and worshipping God and Jesus—is to get to see the ripple effects of all that God has planned for each woman who reads this book. As God works in your life and changes you, I would love to hear from you. I hope you will share your story with me at www.peacefulwife.com in the comments. Maybe I'll have a chance to share your story next. Perhaps God desires to bless and impact hundreds or thousands of women around the world through what He does in your life! That would be just like our amazing God, to use the trials, pain, and suffering you have experienced to bless your family and many others for His Kingdom. May God richly bless your walk with Christ, my sister. You are in my prayers. I am thrilled to be on this road together with you. Thankfully, we don't have to walk this road alone.

Reaching a Husband Who Doesn't Know Christ

Just as you are, your husband is responsible for his own soul and actions. It is the Holy Spirit's responsibility to bring conviction and repentance to your husband. You need to let God and your husband handle the weight of your husband's sin and decisions. Focus on your own obedience to Christ. The closer you are to God—the more you obey Him, feast on His Word, pray for Him to change you, and allow God's Spirit to empower you—the better!

Before you look over the following list, spend some time in prayer. Praise God for who He is and for placing you where you are right now. Confess any known sin. And then, with words like these, commit yourself and your marriage to God's care:

Jesus,

As long as I have You, Your Spirit, and Your Word, I have more than I need. I trust You to provide for my every need in our marriage and for our children. I only seek Your glory in my life no matter what the personal cost to me. I am willing to obey You. Show me how to bless my husband. Open his eyes, Lord.

Bring him to Yourself in Your way, Your power, Your timing, and
for Your glory. I pray most of all for my husband's salvation and
for You to regenerate his spirit and give him new life in Christ.
I pray for healing for him spiritually, for our marriage, and for
every stronghold of the enemy to be torn down.
    In Jesus' name, amen

Now consider these suggestions for respecting your unbelieving or spiritually wounded husband:

- Do not allow the marriage, your husband, or his salvation to become more important to you than Christ. Hold these things all loosely, and cling to Jesus alone. Desire Jesus more than anything else; this is so key!
- Don't talk about spiritual things generally. First Peter 3:1–2 is your assignment from God in this situation until God changes things.
- Be as sensitive as possible to God's nudging by staying in prayer, repenting of any known sin in your own life, reading God's Word, and desiring Him above everything else. Stay very close to God.
- Seek to desire the same things God desires for your husband, not from selfish motives and how much better things would be for you if your husband came to Christ, but because you love your husband with God's love and want God's best for your husband.
- Ask God to show you how to bless and honor your husband.
- Lay down your expectations of your husband and marriage on the altar before God in your heart, releasing your husband to God's care.
- Make no demands. Trust God with your needs right now.
- Show your husband that you genuinely accept him.
- Ask him about things he is interested in, if he is willing to talk about them.

- Use a friendly tone of voice, pleasant facial expressions, and welcoming, positive body language; these are all very important.
- Smile a real smile at him whenever you see him to bless him. Do not be discouraged about his lack of response. Seek to simply "water his soul."
- Hum or sing happily sometimes.
- Thank him for working to provide for the family, if he is doing that.
- Smile and cheerfully say, "Have a great time!" or "Have fun!" when he leaves to be with friends, go to the races, or go to a game.
- Instruct your children to be as respectful as possible when he comes home.
- Do some things you enjoy for yourself.
- Send him a brief text every few days or once a week telling him you are proud of him and why. Expect nothing in return.
- Thank him sincerely for his leadership whenever he makes any decisions for the good of the family.
- Praise him for his good parenting when he is involved with the children.
- Don't talk about the marriage or ask where he is emotionally. Don't try to get him to give you some kind of verbal guarantee for the future. That will often repel him like nothing else. Focus on today as Christ exhorted us to do and let tomorrow worry about itself (Matt. 6:34).
- Be joyfully available sexually to him if possible, unless he is involved in unrepentant adultery or unrepentant pornography use, or you have serious pain or illness, etc. (1 Cor. 7:1–5).
- If you have a godly, trustworthy female prayer partner, ask for prayer. Be prayerful and cautious about how much detail you share with anyone else—and only share serious matters with someone who is spiritually mature and living for Christ herself, who wants to help you focus on what you can do on your side of

the marriage. If there are really serious matters, please *do* share that with a trusted counselor in detail; don't hide what is really happening from him or her; allow the counselor to help you.

- If you need help, try to get help from a godly, biblical counselor (preferably a female if it is just for you, but maybe a male if both of you are going). You may even want to ask your husband if he would be willing to get godly counseling. If he will not go, see if it is possible for you to go if you are in over your head with problems. If you are not safe, please get somewhere safe as soon as possible.
- Be receptive to your husband's suggestions, advice, and ideas if he is not asking you to sin.
- If he asks you to spend time with him, try to go and enjoy him even if it does not involve talking.
- Ask him if there is anything he would like you to do for him.

Let him see that you are totally joyful and content in Christ because you truly *are* joyful and content in Christ alone. This has to be for real.

Read this Christian brother's wisdom on the value of actions over words:

Men are creatures of action, which is a reason why your behavior—not your words—will win him over. If you can't back up your words with actions, you will get no respect in a man's world. Another key point is if you try to preach, teach, and nag your husband to church or to salvation, his salvation will literally be accomplished by his submitting to his wife. That is a very upside-down way to get him into the Kingdom that will yield . . . bad fruit. However, if by your actions you model the love of Christ and show him respect . . . I can guarantee that will have a profound impact and then *he* will choose to come to Christ by making his own decision based on your testimony. Our flesh wants to take the easy way—and it's a whole lot easier to preach at someone than it is to live out the sermon. Living it takes dying daily to ourselves, and that's not easy, but it's the only way for there to be any chance at all.

If a wife's change in Christ is real, this will blow a man's mind. He won't know what to think and will become very curious about how you could possibly have such peace even when he may not be the best husband. He may try to get you to lash out at him. Be prepared for that. He may try to get you to sin against him so that he can focus on your sin again. When you aren't sinning against him anymore, but are obeying Romans 12:9–21, he may start to feel heavy conviction from God's Spirit. That will force him to look at his own issues. If he can get you to sin, then he can justify his own sin again and blame you for the problems in the marriage. Don't take that bait! The only thing your sin can do is create more destruction and damage. Keep obeying God and repay evil with good. Let God work in his heart. If you continue in the power of God's Spirit, then you have the power of heaven at your disposal to breathe hope, healing, life, and blessing into your marriage and your husband's life.

Sheryl's Story

Bert never came home in the middle of a workday. So I was surprised when the back door opened and he walked in last April.

"We need to talk," he said.

"Is your mom all right?" I asked. We recently moved his 96-year-old mom to be near us.

"She's fine. Have a seat."

I was curious, and was a little excited about the prospect of whatever he wanted to discuss. During the years, we talked of many plans for our future. So I thought maybe we were about to begin building our house on the beach. Or maybe he was about to tell me someone was interested in buying his physical therapy practice, so he could semi-retire.

"I want a divorce."

His words cut. An immediate knot formed in the pit of my stomach. Bert stood in our den and counted on his fingers the reasons he could no longer tolerate being married to me. And each time he pointed to a finger to recite another reason, I felt the words slice right into my heart. "And worst of all, I'm tired of your nagging, Sheryl! I'm sick of hearing what I should eat or how much I should read my Bible. I'm through with this marriage!" He plopped into his recliner, breathing heavily, trying to catch his breath. I knew Bert was waiting for me to say something, but my throat was too tightened with emotions. My entire face turned hot and my eyes filled with tears. I couldn't look at him any longer so I stared at my lap until I could regain my voice.

"Oh my gosh, Bert, you're right." That was all I could get out. Over the last several years I knew I was becoming more and more critical. But I also remembered the countless times I *begged* God to help me to change. And now it was too late. We talked a little more and he told me his plan: We would remain in the house we were currently living in (but separate bedrooms) for one month. He figured that would give me enough time to find an apartment near my children in Louisiana. Before he left to return to work, his voice changed to a kinder tone. I could tell he was trying to be supportive in an ironic sort of way. Once he was gone, I gave in to the tears—and panic. I wasn't as worried about what would become *of* me as much as what I *had become.*

For a while, I had been noticing how critical and angry I had been acting, especially when I felt rejected by Bert. The bad behavior and attitudes were so constant that it felt as if they were being added to my character DNA. I can't tell you how much I prayed to stop my disrespectful behavior! Now, I felt as if it wasn't just my marriage that was in danger, but I was also questioning my behavior as an Imitator of Christ. Was I able to change? It looked as if I had only thirty days (before I had to leave) to find out. *God, please give me a second chance. Change me!*

When Bert came home very late that evening, I asked him if I could speak with him. He sat in his chair. "Yes. But I've made up my mind. I want a divorce."

Tears sprang from my eyes again, but I pressed on. "I know, but I want to say something." I sat on the floor and looked into his eyes. "Bert, I know I've messed up. I am asking for a second chance. I'm not asking you to change. Right now, let me do all the changing." (I was amazed at those words coming out of my mouth. Obviously, God was already hard at work!)

"I don't care how much you do change. I'm not changing my mind."

"Okay. But I'm still going to try."

I found some Christian books about respect and forgiveness and read several testimonies from ladies who described their disrespectful behavior toward their respective husbands. I felt shame as I saw myself in many of their stories. *Oh, God, no wonder our marriage has gotten so bad!* I realized I wasn't totally responsible for the demise of my marriage, but I couldn't deny my contributions. The more I read the books, the more I could see how my constant criticism (including the tone of my voice and rolling my eyes) undermined my husband. I cried into my hands as I repented again for my angry, spiteful, and self-righteous heart. Before the day ended, I made memory cards with verses on forgiveness.

As I began to practice God's principles, I started to behave and think differently. Instead of nagging Bert to eat healthy, I bought food I knew he liked. Instead of lecturing him about going to church or having a quiet time, I remained quiet and prayed for him. The house, which was always impossible for me to keep up before, now stayed neat and tidy. And when he came home (later and later each night), I made sure I was pretty. Most importantly, with God's help, I chose to forgive Bert for his failures, and continued to take responsibility for mine. I didn't do any of these things perfectly, but my repentance was real. As I prayed constantly and meditated on God's Word every day, I could sense God's presence penetrating my sadness, even at night while still crying alone in our bed. But hope was returning and I became more aware of God's powerful love for me. Thankfully, I was able to find my significance in Jesus—not in Bert's opinion of me. Therefore, I was able to resist temptation more often; and choose behaviors that pleased God—and Bert. God continued to give me grace to behave like the wife Bert thought he married.

Then one incredible evening, I saw tears in *Bert's* eyes. "Sheryl, I never had anyone love me like you do. I never had someone who was willing to stay with me, in spite of my selfish, self-centered behavior." He reached for my hand and pulled me closer to him. "Will you forgive me?"

I couldn't believe what I was hearing! Then I saw him get his wedding ring from the top of his dresser (where it had been sitting since April). He was about to put it on his finger, but I stopped him. "Hon, may I please place it on your finger?" I saw more tears form in his eyes as he nodded. Thus, a new, sweeter—more loving and respectful—marriage began.

Now Bert and I are *both* becoming the spouses we always wanted to be. He asked me to forgive him for the years of rejection, and I asked him to forgive my years of disrespectful behavior. God used the devastating conversation on April 1 to change my behavior—and our marriage.

As we continue to apply what we learned, Bert and I candidly admit we have not arrived. We are a work in progress for sure! However, we are pleased to report: forgiving, loving, and respecting each other is much easier today than when our journey first began.

From Karen

I was raised in a very strict Christian denomination and was taught that men needed to be the leaders of the home and that women needed to be in submission and quiet in the church—with a huge stress on modesty for women. Those things are all good, but it was taken to the extreme of legalism. I met the love of my life when I was 19. We sinned when we were dating, and I got pregnant. We were required to confess before the church and then got married. I knew nothing about money, how to save or spend wisely, etc. Over the course of the next 10 years, we lived above our means, accumulating tax debt and credit card debt while I stayed at home with our children. We were very active in our church, became youth leaders, sang in the praise group every Sunday, and served on the deacon board. I was dissatisfied with the amount of money my husband made and undermined his authority with our children constantly. I felt he was too hard on our children and would go behind his back to counteract him.

I fully accept and acknowledge my terrible and sinful ways. About seven years ago, I developed thyroid issues, and life got rough. I became a different person. After my health got straightened out, there was hurt and debris left from that storm. My husband felt so alone, became friends with another woman, and began to confide in her. They had an emotional affair. He stopped, but I sensed it was far from over. We had grown apart. He had a lot of bitterness from my years of disrespect for him. We went for a few sessions of counseling. After my husband's first emotional affair, God met me right where I was in all my sin and agony.

Forgiveness—what a powerful thing. I could feel my husband was just putting in time until our children were gone and out of the home. I didn't know what to do about it. So I turned to God, constantly surrendering—taking my burdens to the foot of the cross. I began to pray, "Change me Lord; bless him." We took a money class together. We started to communicate about money, and some healing began. I started working part-time to help with our bills and debt, but I sensed that my husband was still in a war. Many nights I would crawl out of bed, kneel, and pray with my arms lifted up, giving my husband to

God. I pleaded with God to give me a hunger for Him. I experienced so much healing by fully accepting the love that God has for me, that only God can fill that empty spot in my heart. He wants me. He desires me. He never ever gets tired of me.

During all of this, I sensed my husband was not being faithful, but I didn't know to what extent. I had given him to God. He belongs to God first. God brought me to the reality that I am not accountable for my husband's thoughts or his choices. I am responsible for mine. That was freeing. How could I truly love and respect my husband if I wasn't putting God first? When I fully surrendered to the One who loves me so much that He sent His only Son to die for my sins, and accepted the gift He gives us humbly and with constant gratitude, God's healing and work began. As God convicted me and overhauled me, I began to apologize and ask for forgiveness for the disrespect, the dishonesty with money, and other offenses. My husband remained skeptical. I went through all the steps you describe—the wanting to talk about the changes, trying to share with him what was happening. He would get angry with me and tell me to be quiet.

When I went quiet, he began to hear the voice of God. Earlier in the week, when we were laying in bed, he told me that he needed to talk about something. He shared that a woman he knew had called him, saying that her husband was going crazy and going to come tell me that they were having an affair. He confessed that they had texted very inappropriate messages to each other. I didn't get angry; I just listened to him talk. . . . Last night, it all came to a head. He asked me out to dinner and said he needed to talk. He confessed to an affair last summer. He sobbed and said that he had given up hope ten years ago, and was just putting in his time until the kids left. But he said that the way I began to change in front of him—the openness and confessions I was making, seeing with his own eyes a peace and joy that filled me that didn't go away and in fact has been getting stronger—has made him reconsider his choices. We talked for a while, and then I went to bed because I needed space—a place to cry and pour my heart out to God. I was sad, but in awe because God has been preparing me for this. Six months ago, God very clearly spoke to me out loud, and gave me three words to cling to: *in His time.* I had been crying out to God, asking how far this all would have to go for my husband to break. God whispered to me, "Pretty far, but I will never leave you, nor forsake you. I am always with you. . . . " I clung to that promise every day. My husband is a good man, a hard-working family man. I believed in that promise, never giving up hope.

When my husband came to bed, we talked again for a while and then both said at the same time, "Can we pray?" That man I love with all my heart—always have and always will—prayed a prayer that I have been waiting for and beseeching God to hear. He prayed that God would be the center of our marriage, that we would never lose that vision as we walk forward from here, starting over again after twenty years of misunderstanding, hurt, dishonesty, and unfaithfulness. I am so thankful this morning for a God who goes before us, that we cannot rush His timeline and that He loves and forgives us. I am so thankful for a God who stopped me in my tracks, and is overhauling our marriage, my husband, and me. My husband shared with me that when I told him that God had convicted me, and said seventy times seven you must forgive, he knew he must come clean for us to heal and rebuild. There is so much good. My God is with me in the storm, for I have a peace that only He can give. I'm praying that God will show us if we need more counseling, that He will reveal to my husband if we do. I have left that decision up to [my husband]. I am placing my trust in God that He will continue to bring healing and that if my husband needs a mentor, God will bring that person into his life—because He is just that awesome and caring. He has been so faithful to me over and over that how can I question what comes? I must stress that complete surrender to God must happen for wives to be able to make this journey.

And lastly, here is a reminder that God works not only in believers' lives, but in the lives of unbelievers, as well. Katy, the writer of the following story, is married to a man who doesn't know Christ. Recently, God revealed Katy's disrespect toward her husband to her. Her husband is having an affair and has talked about leaving. What God is doing in this wife's heart is miraculous.

Katy's Story

I don't feel like I'm especially growing or learning godliness or wisdom. But I do feel amazed that I am somehow weathering this storm, and it is most definitely not in my own power. I almost hesitate to say it, but I am thankful for what is going on in a way because I know that without this suffering, I would still be blissfully (and ignorantly) drifting along in my life as a casual Christian. I am in awe of how much God's Word speaks to me now. It never did before! I read the Bible before. I memorized so many Scripture passages. I grew up with it and it's been the background music in my life. I don't think I've ever really heard the words before. I just mindlessly hummed along to the tune now and then. Now it's like my life is the background music (as un-harmonious as it is right now) and God's Word is the main feature! I find myself looking forward to reading my Bible. I've never really felt that before.

My prayer life is growing. It has a long way to go and it doesn't seem to be an easy practice for me, but I have the desire to seek and know God in ways I never had before. It's exciting! God is real and meaningful in ways I've never experienced before through His Word and through the sense of calm I have in this storm. I can so feel how this calmness is directly related to where my focus is, too. If my eyes are on Him, it's amazingly peaceful despite the chaos around me—but when my eyes start focusing on myself (hurt feelings, etc.), my husband, or even on good things (my children)—then it's impossible not to start sinking into despair at the hopelessness of ever making it through the storm. If God had not brought this brokenness into my life, I would not have been able to see Him. He has blessed me with such good things throughout my life, but it's only in this time of suffering that I have really begun to know that He's there and to grasp how much I really need Him. In general, I think I'm just different than my husband in that regard personality-wise. I also don't get anxious about things the way that my husband does. He seems to experience highs and lows of emotions to a fuller degree than I do. I don't think that's necessarily good or bad, just the way God made us. However, his question, "What are you even passionate about?" has been ringing in my ears and has now become my prayer. I want to be passionate about my relationship with God, and I pray that one day my husband will be able to see that and know what I'm passionate about and want it for himself.

I am so thankful that [April] explained idolatry to me. I had never ever heard it explained that way or understood that it was when we put anyone or anything first in our heart and life above God. I always thought references to idolatry in the Bible were irrelevant. No one has "idols" in our society (ha!). It makes so much more sense now and has gone from being an irrelevant issue to something so vital. I read 1 John the other day. It has such clear descriptions of how others know by our lives if we truly love God and follow Jesus. I am really trying to understand how to reflect Christ in my life to my husband and children, and 1 John is pretty clear about what our lives should look like. Then the final verse ends the book with "Dear children, keep yourselves from idols." My initial reaction was, "What? How random! Was this comment an afterthought? It seems that verse was just stuck on. There's no context for it." Even the comment in my Bible just indicates "idols" are "false gods as opposed to the one true God." What an anticlimactic way to end a great book!

Then it hit me. This is the key. This is what the entire rest of the book hinges on! Unless God is in His rightful place in my heart and life, my first and only priority, there is no way I can do the rest of the things described by 1 John: walk in the light, love my brother, etc. . . . If I have any idols in my life—even "good" ones, like my children or my husband—then I am breaking His command, displeasing Him, and not following Christ's example. If I am living in sin, I am not in Him. I was blown away by this revelation. I have never seen or understood anything so clearly in the Bible before. I know it wasn't my own understanding, but the Holy Spirit revealing truth to me that I'd never before been able to see. This is so exciting! And what power is promised to us in 1 John: He hears and gives us whatever we ask when we are in His will, obeying His command to have no idols before Him in our lives.

Notes

Chapter 2. Finding the Missing Piece of the Puzzle

1. Dr. Emerson Eggerichs, *Love and Respect* (Nashville: Thomas Nelson, 2004), 1.
2. If this is a new concept for you, please search "How to Have a Relationship with Christ" on my home page, www.peacefulwife.com.

Chapter 3. Let's Be Honest

1. "The Danvers Statement" by The Council on Biblical Manhood and Womanhood, in Recovering Biblical Manhood and Womanhood, ed. Wayne Grudem and John Piper (Wheaton, IL: Crossway, 2006), 470.

Chapter 5. God's Beautiful Design

1. Wayne Grudem and John Piper, "Questions and Answers," in *Recovering Biblical Manhood and Womanhood*, ed. Wayne Grudem and John Piper (Wheaton, IL: Crossway, 2006), 61.
2. Ibid., 61–62.
3. For more about this topic, please read Wayne Grudem and John Piper, eds., *Recovering Biblical Manhood and Womanhood* (Wheaton, IL: Crossway, 2006).
4. Grudem and Piper, "Questions and Answers," in *Recovering Biblical Manhood and Womanhood*, 72.
5. David Ayers, "The Inevitability of Failure: The Assumptions and Implementations of Modern Feminism," in *Recovering Biblical Manhood and Womanhood: A Response to Evangelical Feminism*

ed. by John Piper and Wayne Grudem (Wheaton, IL: Crossway, 2006), 321–22.

6. Ibid.

7. E. M. Bounds, *The Classic Collection on Prayer* (Alachua, FL: Bridge-Logos, 2001), 61.

Chapter 7. Acknowledging Our Sin

1. Nina Roesner, *The Respect Dare* (Nashville: Thomas Nelson, 2012). This was previously published in 2009 by iUniverse.

2. Shaunti Feldhahn, *For Women Only* (Colorado Springs: Multnomah, 2004, 2013).

Chapter 8. My Husband Shares His Heart

1. Dr. Laura Schlessinger, *The Proper Care and Feeding of Husbands* (New York: HarperCollins, 2004); Laura Doyle, *The Surrendered Wife* (New York: Fireside, 2001).

Chapter 11. Communicating Our Desires Respectfully

1. See, e.g., "Three Important Times to NOT Speak . . ." The Respect Dare blog, accessed October 15, 2015, http://ninaroesner .com/2015/01/22/three-reasons-keep-quiet/.

2. See, e.g., "Angry & Married & Doing Something About It—With the Smaller Things . . ." The Respect Dare blog, accessed October 15, 2015, http://ninaroesner.com/2011/01/19/angry-married-doing-something-about-it-with-the-smaller-things/.

3. Laura Doyle, *The Surrendered Wife* (New York: Simon and Schuster, 1999), 86, 228.

Chapter 12. Respecting Our Husbands During Conflict

1. Shaunti Feldhahn, *For Women Only* (Colorado Springs: Multnomah, 2004, 2013).

For Further Study

Cobb, Nancy, and Connie Grigsby. *The Politically Incorrect Wife.* Colorado Springs: Multnomah, 2002. Two wives join together to describe biblical submission from a Christian and practical perspective.

Doyle, Laura. *The Surrendered Wife.* New York: Fireside, 2001. This book helped me work through my world-influenced thoughts and find new ways to think, speak, and act that were respectful. It is not written from a Christian perspective, so readers will need to carefully weigh what is shared against biblical truth.

Easley, Cindy. *Dancing with the One You Love.* Chicago: Moody, 2010. A Christian wife interviews wives in unique situations about how biblical submission plays out in their circumstances—military wives, talk-show hosts, unbelieving husbands, chronically ill husbands, and so on.

Eggerichs, Emerson. *Love and Respect.* Nashville: Thomas Nelson, 2004. This is a Christian book that describes what husbands and wives uniquely need in marriage and gives spouses a place to start to learn how to love and respect each other.

Feldhahn, Shaunti. *For Women Only.* Colorado Springs: Multnomah, 2004, 2013. Written from a Christian perspective, this book helped me understand how men think and feel and opened up the world of masculinity to me.

Kimmel, Tim. *Grace Filled Marriage.* Brentwood, TN: Worthy, 2013. A Christian book for husbands and wives about extending grace in practical ways in marriage. There is a powerful chapter about how wives can give grace to husbands who have been ensnared by pornography.

Larimore, Walt, and Barb Larimore. *His Brain, Her Brain*. Grand Rapids: Zondervan, 2008. A look at the differences in the brains of men and women from a Christian neuroscientist's perspective.

Mahaney, Carolyn. *Feminine Appeal: Seven Virtues of a Godly Wife and Mother*. Wheaton, IL: Crossway, 2004, 2012. A Christian wife expounds on the qualities of a Titus 2:3–5 wife. This is a wonderful study on godly femininity.

McCulley, Carolyn. *Radical Womanhood: Feminine Faith in a Feminist World*. Chicago: Moody, 2008. A former feminist turned Christian takes us on a journey through the history of feminism over the past two decades, exploring how culture's definition of femininity, masculinity, and marriage has been greatly impacted. McCulley presents biblical womanhood in practical ways.

Peace, Martha. *The Excellent Wife: A Biblical Perspective*. Bemidji, MN: Focus, 2005. A powerful resource for Christian wives to learn to allow God to transform their thinking as women and as wives.

Piper, John and Wayne Grudem, eds. *Recovering Biblical Manhood and Womanhood*. Wheaton, IL: Crossway, 2006. A compilation of more than twenty authors' works addressing feminism in the church and what it means to be biblical men and women and to have biblical marriages. The first edition of this book (1991) is available free at http://www.cbmw.org/resources/.

Roesner, Nina. *The Respect Dare*. Nashville: Thomas Nelson, 2012. A forty-day guide to beginning to understand what it means to respect your husband from a Christian perspective with daily assignments for wives.

Thomas, Gary. *Sacred Influence*. Grand Rapids: Zondervan, 2006. A masculine Christian perspective on how wives can most impact their husbands for Christ. The second half of the book has powerful examples and real-life stories dealing with infidelity, husbands with anger issues, and various types of conflict.

White, Jennifer O. *Prayers for New Brides*. Green Forest, AR: New Leaf, 2015. A fantastic resource and prayer guide for brides of all ages as they pray for themselves, their husbands, and their marriages.

About the Author

April has two blogs, http://www.peacefulwife.com for married women and http://www.peacefulsinglegirl.wordpress.com for unmarried women. Her goal is to be a Titus 2:3–5 mentor, teaching women to love God wholeheartedly and to allow Him to transform them to be the women He desires them to be. April also has a YouTube channel, "April Cassidy," where she has many videos about being a godly wife.

Nothing brings April greater joy than to see God work in people's lives and to hear the stories of miracles He has done in their marriages and families. She believes she has found "the pearl of greatest price" in Christ, and she can't wait to share this good news with everyone she can!

APRIL CASSIDY

The
Peaceful
Mom

Building a healthy foundation with

Christ AS Lord